Strong Enough

What it Takes for a Church to Thrive in a Godless Culture

Jeff Kliewer

Strong Enough: What it Takes for a Church to Thrive in a Godless Culture

Italics in biblical quotes indicate emphasis added.

Unless otherwise indicated, all Scripture quotations are from: The Holy Bible, English Standard Version, copyright 2001 by Crossway Bibles, a division of Good News Publishers. Used by permission. All rights reserved.

Cover design: Chrysta Hooper

First printing, 2017

Printed in the United States of America

ISBN: 0692940499
ISBN-13: 978-0692940495

DEDICATION

To the church that entrusted the pulpit to me. I tremble at the responsibility, but trust that God's strength will be made perfect in my weakness. My deep desire for us is that we be built together upon Christ into a spiritual house that lives always and entirely for His glory.

CONTENTS

Acknowledgments   I

Introduction   1

1   Strong Members   9

2   Strong Teaching   27

3   Strong Theology   45

4   Strong Gifts   67

5   Strong Love   87

Conclusion   103

ACKNOWLEDGMENTS

I owe a tremendous debt of gratitude to the 5 pastors who contributed to this book or were featured in it. Mark Willey, Bob Spicer, Warren Boettcher, Bill Luebkemann, and Marty Berglund are fellow workers in Christ's building project—the formation of the Church. They are also fellow travelers on the road of ministry. They minister in their local churches, yet remembering that it is really only one Church that each of us serves, they took the time to help with this project, desiring to see other churches thrive, even as their own churches continue to thrive. Their Kingdom mindset deserves to be acknowledged.

INTRODUCTION

This house is strong. Here in Florida, summer afternoons usually bring fierce thunderstorms. There's one rolling in right now as I write. Looking out a bay window, I can see two palm trees. The wind is bending them half way over. The branches look like the hair of a woman on a rollercoaster, pulled straight back by the wind. Lightning flashes every ten seconds or so. And the thunder clap is only a second behind, which means the bolts are very close to me. But I don't have the slightest concern. I am staying in a well-built house.

Well-built churches have nothing to fear when the storms come. Build a church on the Rock Christ Jesus, using the right materials, and it will stand up against the trials of life. Christ is the Cornerstone— the solid rock on which we stand. He will never fail. But what materials are we using to build on Him? We

1

might be able to prop up a house of hay and stubble. But as soon as a storm comes, the house will fall. What then makes for a well-built church?

The storm is here. Secular humanism is blowing across the Western world with the force of a hurricane. Much of what the Church has built has already been laid waste. Most of Europe is a religious wasteland. America has held up better, but the trends aren't looking good.

What does it take for a church to stand in a godless culture? Moreover, what does it take for a church to *thrive* in such an environment? That is the question that gave birth to this book.

The question looms large in my mind because I recently became the pastor of an Evangelical Free church in New Jersey. Before that, I was a missionary for 12 years in a rough part of Philadelphia. During that time, we worked to help establish 3 churches. The dangers in the city included rampant drug culture, violence, and everything else that comes with the breakdown of the family. But secular humanism was at the root, just as it is in the suburbs.

A few years ago, we moved to a New Jersey suburb and I commuted to inner city Philadelphia to do my missionary work. But one evening, I went for a jog near my house. I ran past an Evangelical Free church and prayed for her. As I finished my run, I walked past the house of a man I knew to be an elder of that church. So, I prayed another short prayer for the church. As I did, I received a text message (I always carry my phone when I run). It said that this very church was "interested in talking to you about pulpit supply". I replied that I had been "praying for their church right when you texted". I took that "coincidence" as a sign that I better agree to preach.

One thing led to another. My family and I absolutely loved the church, and the church evidently liked us well enough, because a few months later, the church called on me to be their pastor. For me, it was a joyful display of God's sovereignty, and humorous, because that friend who texted me now began to call me "Reverend". He even put a "Clergy" license plate holder on my car, making fun of me, because he knew I hated titles like that. I drove around with a moronic "Clergy" license plate for days before I saw what he did.

So, although I have been in full-time ministry since 2000, I am new to the role of Senior Pastor. And everything in me wants to see this church thrive. Therefore, I set out on a quest to discover what it takes. I know that Jesus Christ is the unchanging Rock upon which we are to build. But how do we build well upon that unshakable foundation? Wood, hay and stubble won't do. We have to be strong enough to overcome the godless culture that seeks to tear people away from the church and level the church to the ground. I turned to two major sources: Scripture and five pastors who have been building here for years.

My study of the Scriptures centered in two places. First, I read and reread the book of Acts. I looked for major themes. I tried to hear Luke's voice, as well as his intention. "What are you doing with what you are saying?", I asked the author. Ultimately, I was asking God to show me the key themes of the book He inspired. Second, I examined passages that speak of Christ as "the Cornerstone" (Luke 20, Ephesians 2, Acts 4, Psalm 95, 1 Peter 2). If Christ is the Rock on which we are to build, what do these passages teach about how to build on Him? Then, I reached out to 5 pastors.

I used to want to be like Mike. Now I want to be like Mark. And Bob, Warren, Bill, and Marty. Michael Jordan built a name for himself on the basketball court. These guys built churches, not for themselves, and not by themselves, but for and by the Name that is above every name.

Pastor Mark founded Fellowship Community (Baptist) Church in 1981. Pastor Bob began building Grace Bible Church in 1970. Pastor Warren started a Sovereign Grace Church in 1993. Pastor Bill began a Calvary Chapel in 1997. Pastor Marty founded Fellowship Alliance Chapel in 1980.

This book is the result of a listening effort…me learning from them. And I am very pleased to pass on what they had to say. Each chapter of this book contains an essay from one of the pastors, or an interview or story, all new material released here for the first time. I am truly grateful for the contributions of these pastors.

The 5 churches they pastor are quite different from each other. None of them belong to the same denomination. There are significant doctrinal distinctions between them. There are differences in church government. In membership size, they range from medium to mega. They use different methods to do ministry. One of them founded a radio station that broadcasts the gospel from Baltimore to New Jersey.

Yet I would say that all of these churches are thriving. So, in light of the differences between the churches, allow me to define my terms. I don't mean *perfect* or *ideal* when I say *thriving*. To be a *thriving* church, she needs to be both *true* and *growing*.

A *true* church is evangelical in the biblical sense. The Greek word *eungelion* gives us *evangel*, meaning "good news", which, in turn, gives us our English word "gospel". A true church has the biblical gospel. She preaches Christ, and Him crucified and risen.

A *growing* church is one that is expanding in three directions. It is growing larger in numbers, either by new people joining the local church or by church planting and missionary activity worldwide that actually increases the number of disciples and local churches on the earth. It is growing deeper in the Word as the Word takes center stage in the pulpit, classrooms and homes. And it is growing wider in love as members of the church develop their relationships with one another, caring for members and those outside the church as well.

To me, a church has to be more than just *true* to be called "thriving". It has to be *growing* 3-dimensionally. If it isn't, it may have the true preaching of the Word and the ordinances rightly administered, but time will see it dwindle.

It is not easy to build a thriving church. In fact, if America is on the same path as Europe, only 50 years or so behind, which appears to be the case, then we live at a particularly difficult time and place. The culture is secularizing. Humanism is rising. Christians are increasingly portrayed as hindrances to "progress". It is hard to build in this environment.

But these 5 churches within 5 miles of the church I pastor *are* thriving. And that—all genuine Christians will agree—is entirely owed to the gracious hand of God. He will build His Church, and apart from Him, we can do nothing. Still, God uses secondary causes to accomplish His purposes. He himself is the only uncaused Cause. He is the primary Mover that accomplishes everything that happens under the sun. Our work is never more than a secondary cause. But thinking on that level, to what can we attribute the thriving of these 5 churches?

For that matter, what makes any church thrive? What's the difference between the thriving church on one corner and the church on the opposite side of the street that is experiencing a *failure to thrive*?

Before going on to that, I need to state two caveats. First, God is sovereign over all. So, He has purposes for everything, including the birth and death of local churches. His secret will is inscrutable, so even though we try to trace out principles about how things function here upon the plane on which we live, we must remember that God will ultimately do as He sees fit to do, notwithstanding whatever principles we seek to employ. So, this book is no knock on dwindling churches. It may be God's will for a church to dwindle for a time, or, as counterintuitive as it sounds, for the church to die. God has allowed local churches to come and go for 2,000 years. This book is no condemnation upon any struggling church. It is, rather, a search for principles and an exhortation to try to employ them, whatever comes of it. We leave the results to God.

Second, I want to avoid the error of becoming overly ecumenical. I don't want to minimize important Biblical teachings on church government, ministry methods, or doctrine. I am so encouraged by the friendships I have with each of the pastors who contributed to this book. I consider them all mentors to me. I am learning a lot from them. But each of us would say the same thing about our differences...they matter. The teachings I have included in this book, from each of these men, are areas where I agree with them. And if on some other points we think differently, in time God will reveal the truth to them :)

The men who contributed to this book were gracious to me. They contributed their insight in areas of our agreement even though they know we probably don't agree on everything. They are not accountable for what others have written, but I stand to be judged for the work as a whole.

Those caveats stated, I may as well lay all of my cards on the table from the outset. I desire to be used of God to build not only a thriving church, but particularly one that is 1) boldly Evangelical, 2) thoroughly Biblical, 3) unapologetically Calvinistic, 4) carefully Charismatic, and 5) passionately Loving. These 5 things aren't just presuppositions I bring with me as baggage when I talk about how to build a thriving church. They are part and parcel of what this book aims to establish. From my perspective, a thriving church, if it is becoming everything it is supposed to be, is becoming all of these things.

By God's grace, I think our church is moving steadily in these directions. Of course, we have a long way to go. But we are part of the bride of Christ and He is constantly reforming us until we are beautifully adorned for presentation unto Him at the Wedding Supper of the Lamb.

Or, to use a more masculine metaphor, we are a building made of living stones. The Builder is still shifting us around and cementing us in where we belong. He is building us together upon the Cornerstone. He is making His church strong. Strong members (boldly Evangelical), strong teaching (thoroughly Biblical), strong theology (unapologetically Calvinistic), strong gifts (carefully Charismatic), and strong love (passionately Loving) are the building blocks of a thriving church.

1. STRONG MEMBERS

"But he looked directly at them and said, "What then is this that is written: 'The stone that the builders rejected has become the cornerstone'?" (Luke 20:17)

The biggest detriment to the thriving of a church is the presence of too many unregenerate voices in the choir. If the gathered assembly on Sunday morning has too many goat voices interspersed with the sheep voices, or if the choir of voices in the board room includes even one unregenerate voice, let alone the voice of a wolf in sheep's clothing (Matthew 7:15), the church is in grave danger of failing.

A *failure to thrive* is usually less about what a church lacks and more about having something toxic within the system. The church is not the building, but imagine if it were. If a large number of the cement blocks were actually made of packed sand, wouldn't much of the building disappear with the first heavy rain? Wouldn't the structure eventually fail? Or if asbestos was used for insulation, how long would the Inspector allow that to stand? Likewise, if too many unbelievers are speaking out in church gatherings, or if the things that come out of the mouths of even some believing members are toxic darts, the church will be crumbly and sick. Why would God make her stand, let alone thrive?

It's not only unregenerate members who are toxic to the system. Genuine believers are prone to fall back into worldly thought patterns (hence the imperative not to do so in Romans 12:2) and introduce dangerous toxins into the life of the church. One divisive person, if their voice is loud enough, can stunt the growth of a church. Thriving churches are built with converted, consecrated, and consistent members. So, how do we get those? And how do we rid ourselves of toxins?

Pastor Mark Willey began a Bible study in his home in 1981. It grew to become the Fellowship Community Church of today. Here are his thoughts about developing strong members.

Pastor Mark Willey, Fellowship Community Church

One of my favorite baptism candidates was a 50 year old, tough, seasoned cop. As he stood in the baptismal tank sharing his story of faith, he said, "I just decided I needed to quit talking the talk and start walking the walk". Following Jesus requires walking the walk. Jesus was to the point when identifying people of real faith. It is the mom, dad, son, daughter who "denies himself and takes up his cross and follows me" (Matthew 16:24).

I've served at the same church for over 35 years. My wife and I started this church. No one can tell me, "We used to do it this way!!!" But, I can't blame my predecessor for any of our problems and weaknesses either. I have had a hand in all of them. All came under my watch. We walk as a broken people with a help-giving God.

But, I do thank God for the many, beautiful people at FCC that are humbly seeking to "walk the walk". I often feel that happens in spite of the plans and energies of we Pastors to empower that journey. God does it. Years of ministry have caused me to have far less confidence in my ability to help people walk the walk. But, it has given me far more confidence that God creatively does so. And it seems to me that the church's need is to seek an atmosphere that supports rather than hinders the Spirit of God in that work. There are certain things that we can value that encourage people to be serious minded in their pursuit of Christ. We can...

Value heart level change.

Jesus continually aimed to focus people on their hearts. This is where Jesus directed people who wanted to change. Everything in our lives flows out of our heart (Proverbs 4:23). Our words, our actions, our body language… all comes from what is going on inside of us. The best external church members in Jesus' day (Pharisees) were the most destructive to His cause. They did not know their motives, the ambitions that ruled their hearts, and the internal idols that they gave their lives to serving. Our People Helping People course (a year-long course) is built on discovering your own heart idols, tracing your relational/personal conflicts to heart idols. When you can do it with yourself, you can help others. I loved the lady, a Christian of many years who said, "Before I took this course, I didn't even know I had a heart!". The Puritans (1600s) talked about the importance of "self knowledge". Knowing our hearts and dealing with our hearts leads to deeper hunger for Christ and the power only He has to bring about real change.

Value those who are cast on God in desperation.

We have a ministry known as Celebrate Recovery. It is a recovery ministry with a Christ-centered foundation. Sometimes people get the idea that a recovery ministry is for people with special issues or struggles. But, all of us are in recovery. The fall did that to us. We are broken, marred beings who are in the process of recovering from the horrific influence of sin. We are people desperate for God the Healer. Being transparent about our desperation is the church's greatest glory. We boast in our weakness, our utter need of Christ. Desperate people are committed people. They come to church not out of duty or habit. They come because they hunger to be with others who are saying, "It is true… God is real… He IS changing lives… He is changing me!"

Value the body's role in holiness.

I believe in church membership. Not to get a vote. Not to identify with the brand. But, to covenant together. The covenant in which we agree to be held accountable for our behavior, our beliefs, our relationships, is the only way that the beautiful gift of accountability is ultimately exercised by the body. I just heard last week of a 5th national case where someone living in sin sued a church and won, because they tried to lovingly exercise discipline toward them. In each case, the plaintiff was not a member. In each case, the court determined that the individual had not "covenanted" or "agreed" with the church's position on sexual expression, or gossip, etc. Without membership there was no ultimate accountability. Most real accountability, of course, takes place in private relationships, in small groups in the body, but corporate discipline when exercised with humility and love supports a culture of holy accountability.

Value being responders more than initiators.

One of our Core Values is "We seek to keep in step with the Spirit". That needs to be modelled by the leaders, the influencers of our body. It means that those wired as Initiators, take charge people, come to grips with the reality that spiritual leadership is different than anything else. You are never the final decision maker. You are always a responder listening to Someone else telling you what to do. It means that every ministry needs to be started by the will of the Holy Spirit. But, every ministry then must be allowed to die, in the Spirit's time. Every ministry has an expiration date. We teach this principle in our Core Classes, including membership class. Things have to be allowed to expire if we are keeping in step with the Spirit.

Value those who know that growth is always change.

I have such respect for people that have been at our church for many years and are the biggest cheerleaders of the next generation. They don't see change as a disregard of the past, but the opportunity to see God in new ways, new places. Every area of growth in our lives involves change. It is what growth is. If you don't allow change as a corporate value, you are not growing spiritually or numerically.

God alone makes strong church members. But, we can encourage an atmosphere that supports His work.

Thank you, Pastor Mark, for your encouraging words.

Cornerstone Strong—Luke 20

Luke 20 presents us with the picture of a sick assembly, a crumbling structure. When Jesus arrived in the Temple, He exposed the malady. The leadership of Israel assumed that their authority was authentic (Luke 20:1-2), but long ago, they stopped listening to the authoritative word of God (Luke 20:3-8). So, Jesus gives a word from God to the bystanders, and it was less than encouraging to the leaders of Israel (Luke 20:9-18).

Jesus tells a parable about tenants of a vineyard who reject the authority of the vineyard's owner. So brazen is their rejection of authority that they turn violent against the owner's representatives. As if that were not enough, they then conspire, and kill the owner's Son! So, they ought to expect the owner's wrath to fall upon them in due time.

Now, before hearing this parable, the leaders had resorted to giving Jesus the silent treatment. In truth, they simply had no good answer when Jesus questioned them about the words of John the Baptist (20:7). Still, they undoubtedly held their noses high in their silence, pretending themselves to be above the need to answer this itinerant rabbi. But when they heard this parable, understanding it to be about them, they broke their self-righteous silence (awkward as it was in the first place) to blurt out an unimpressive response. "Surely not!" (Luke 20:16) was all they could come up with.

As they shifted and squirmed, unable to amplify their argument with anything more than their mere assertion "surely not", Jesus "looked directly at them". He addressed them with the very thing these usurpers were rejecting. He confronted them with the authoritative Word of God.

"But he looked directly at them and said, "What then is this that is written: "'The stone that the builders rejected has become the cornerstone'? Everyone who falls on that stone will be broken to pieces, and when it falls on anyone, it will crush him" (Luke 20:17-18).

Jesus quotes Psalm 118:22, identifying Himself as the prophesied "cornerstone". He then intensifies that claim with a condemnation of those who reject His authority. He derives much of the wording from Isaiah 8:14-15, but now bluntly makes Himself the issue and the Jewish leaders the first in line to fall. "Everyone who falls on that stone", the stone being *the Person of Jesus Christ*, "will be broken to pieces", i.e. *judged and punished severely*, "and when it falls on anyone", meaning that *Jesus is the one doing the judging,* "it will crush him", the outcome being *eternal irreversible punishment.*

Those who finally rebel against the authority of Jesus, as His will is revealed in the Scriptures, are devoted to destruction. That is the point of Luke 20:1-18. And it has at least three applications for churches that desire to thrive. We must build with materials 1) that have been converted, 2) that are consecrated, and 3) that will remain consistent. We must build with something other than toxic materials devoted to destruction. A thriving church is built with strong members—converted, consecrated, and consistent.

Converted

Half of the churches in America are mere social clubs. Back in the day, they were born from gospel witness. But the glory has departed. People still gather on Sunday mornings, but it is a mixture of believers with unbelievers. Some still come to worship the true and living God, but others are there to see their friends, bake cookies, plays cards, or give their kids a little religion, because, their thinking goes, "a little religion is good for the kids".

The biggest reason churches fail to thrive is that some of these people—goats among the sheep— make it into leadership. That is why there are entire denominations in America that are 1) compromising the gospel and 2) dwindling year by year. They cave to the culture on gospel issues, like the Bible's authority to define sexual morality, so they anticipate that the culture will love them more. Yet they shrink by 5 percent every year. Their candle stand will soon be removed. Their malady is just what Jesus diagnosed in Luke 20. They have goats, who are devoted to destruction, leading the church.

A thriving church is built with strong members, which means, first of all, that they are genuinely converted. When it comes to ensuring that our people have genuinely been converted, we evangelicals have erred greatly in recent decades. We have neglected the Biblical imperative to "examine yourselves, to see whether you are in the faith..." (2 Corinthians 13:5). We've missed the entire book of First John.

Two reasons come to mind. Our revivalism, stemming from the Second Great Awakening and continuing in Crusade Evangelism, has given us a preoccupation with tallying converts. "Raise your hand if you want to accept Jesus". Then, as soon as we see that hand, we count the convert.

Secondly, and more importantly, we've been more influenced by psychology than we realize. We are so quick to assure people of their salvation, worried as we are about their self-esteem, that we short-circuit the very process that God ordained. Preaching the gospel is meant to make people uncomfortable. Yet we reassure them too quickly, relieving their discomfort. But conviction of sin, when sinners come under it, is actually the kindness of God. We ought to be praying for more conviction, until the person comes to repentance, rather than reassuring them that they are ok, just to protect their self-esteem.

A thriving church is boldly evangelical. The gospel is understood to be a call to repentance and faith (Acts 20:21). Repentance is turning away from sin. The sinner feels genuine contrition and turns their back on what they formerly embraced. Faith is in the Person of Jesus Christ and the work He accomplished by His dying and rising. The sinner now trusts Jesus Christ for forgiveness of sin and eternal life. This is the *eungelion*—the Gospel. Evangelical churches must preach it. Strong members are, first of all, converted.

Consecrated

Those who desire to be strong members of a thriving church should first examine themselves to see if they are in the faith. But assuming they pass the test, they should seek to be fully consecrated unto Christ.

Consecration is sometimes associated with a ritual, such as when a Roman Catholic Priest "consecrates" bread and wine as they perform what they call a "Sacrament". But that's not Biblical consecration. The Bible calls Christians to put *ourselves* upon the altar, to climb up and lay down "as a living sacrifice, holy and acceptable to God, which is your spiritual worship" (Romans 12:1).

Even genuinely converted Christians have a tendency to leave this place of consecration unto Christ and begin to live for ourselves. When we do, we "grieve the Holy Spirit of God, by whom [we] were sealed for the day of redemption" (Ephesians 4:30). When we are in this sad state, our priorities out of whack, we are of little use to God. It's not that He ever needs us. "Whatever the Lord pleases, He does, in heaven and on earth, in the seas and all deeps" (Psalm 135:6). But He is pleased to use those who are pleasing to Him. When we are grieving the Spirit, we become weak and ineffective in the work of the Lord.

A thriving church is made of converted and consecrated members. Consecrated Christians preach the gospel well, with clarity and with boldness. A thriving church will have many strong members who pray like Paul, that "words may be given to me in opening my mouth boldly to proclaim the mystery of the gospel, for which I am an ambassador in chains, that I may declare it boldly, as I ought to speak" (Ephesians 6:19-20). Consecrated Christians are *evangelistic* Christians, and where there is much evangelism, the church is sure to thrive.

So, what inspires genuinely converted Christians to consecrate themselves afresh to serve the Living God? Seeing and savoring Jesus Christ motivates the Christian heart to climb back up onto the altar. After upholding the preeminence of Christ in Colossians 1:15-20, Paul exhorts the Colossian believers to complete consecration. "And you, who once were alienated and hostile in mind, doing evil deeds, he has now reconciled in his body of flesh by his death," that's conversion, "in order to present you *holy and blameless and above reproach* before him", a living sacrifice consecrated unto Him (Colossians 1:21-22). Strong members are consecrated.

Consistent

The third and final thing that makes for a strong member is *consistency*. Thriving churches are built of converted and consecrated Christians (Colossians 1:21-22), but we have to remain that way over time. Paul continues to describe those who belong to the preeminent One this way…"if indeed you continue in the faith, *stable and steadfast*, not shifting from the hope of the gospel that you heard, which has been proclaimed in all creation under heaven, and of which I, Paul, became a minister" (Colossians 1:23).

Anywhere you find a thriving church, you will always see those stalwarts of the faith anchoring the body, giving it stability and steadfastness. From time to time, the flash-in-the-pan type will get fired up and serve passionately for a few months. But it is the consistent ones that demonstrate true strength. Emotion and self-promotion can motivate for a few months, but only the strong can grind on decade after decade. "Where there are no oxen, the manger is clean, but abundant crops come by the strength of the ox" (Proverbs 14:4).

The most obvious need for consistency is simply attending church services, especially on the Lord's Day, the Resurrection Day, Sunday (Revelation 1:10, 1 Corinthians 16:2). Long ago, American culture abandoned the practice of setting aside time for worship. And sadly, many Christians have been conformed to the culture (Romans 12:2) in this regard. Sports, birthday parties, catching up on sleep, or similar pursuits displace the weekly gathering, which exists for the worship of God. "The heavens declare the glory of God" (Psalm 19:1), but we put volleyball ahead of Him! Brothers and sisters, this should never be. Even on vacations, converted consecrated Christians should consistently set aside the Lord's Day to worship the Lord. There are churches in the town you are visiting that would love to have you worship with them that day. And when home, very few things should ever come between you and the assembly for worship. The Scriptures are clear on this point. We are commanded not to "[neglect] to meet together, as is the habit of some" (Hebrews 10:25).

Beyond merely attending services on Sundays, strong members are always serving in some capacity. They have taken on the identity of the voluntary slave, the *doulos* (Romans 1:1, Philippians 1:1). Whether the need be for Sunday School teachers, cooks, cleaners, singers, or set-up/ tear-down personnel, the consistent servant is there and willing to help.

Application

Give me a church of 100 converted consecrated consistent Christians over 100,000 Spirit-grieving sporadic people, half of whom are actually goats, any day! I'll take the smaller but stronger membership. Thriving churches are made of strong members. Numbers will grow from strength, which means the growth will happen the right way. But the starting point is with each individual member. We need to examine ourselves, repent, believe, consecrate ourselves to serve the Living God, and remain this way over time. Then, each of us will be as strong as an ox, and yoked together, God will use us to build a thriving church.

Luke 20 calls us to be *boldly evangelical*. That's what creates strong members. That's also what chases away the goats.

The text addresses us as individuals. Luke 20 draws a line in the sand between believer and unbeliever. Christ the Cornerstone is either the foundation of one's life or the stumbling stone upon which a person falls. If you are reading this and not sure if you stand on Him, then hear the call to conversion. If you genuinely call upon Christ to save you, repenting of your sins, He will do it (Romans 10:13, Acts 2:21). Those who have been converted need to consecrate our lives entirely unto Him. Let go of worldly pursuits, die to those things, and follow Christ. Do this consistently over time.

The text also addresses us as churchmen. Our membership needs to be composed of genuine believers. Before accepting someone as an official member, the elders should hear their testimony and follow up with diagnostic questions, admitting to membership only those who are genuinely believed to be converted. Likewise, the ordinances (Baptism and The Lord's Supper) need to be reserved for genuine Christians. We need to guard the baptismal and the table.

Finally, even as Christ boldly declared Himself to be the Cornerstone, while warning of pending judgment, we need to be boldly evangelistic. Preach the gospel often, with a clear call to repentance. Realize that this will be taken as offensive by a majority of those who live in this secular humanist culture. But do it anyway. Let the Gospel ring out from the pulpit, without watering it down. As the Gospel weeds out unbelievers, it will be a damper on numerical growth. But it will make for healthy growth. And as our members become strong, each of us will become boldly evangelistic in our neighborhoods, workplaces, places of recreation, and everywhere we go. A thriving church is born of the Gospel, so be converted, consecrated, and consistent, proclaiming the Gospel wherever you go.

Discussion Questions

When have you seen toxic behavior in the church that stunted the growth of the church?

What do you and your church need to learn from what Pastor Mark had to say?

Do you think there are many unconverted people who still attend church services regularly in America? What danger comes with that? How do we safeguard against that danger?

Would you say that you are fully consecrated to Jesus Christ right now? What prevents you from climbing up onto the altar today (Romans 12:1)?

How consistent has your walk with Christ been? What changes can you make to be more stable and steadfast (Colossians 1:23)? Who could hold you accountable?

Does your church guard the membership, the baptismal, and the Communion table?

Who in your church reminds you of Paul in how they evangelize (Philippians 3:17, Acts 20:24)? What can you learn from them?

When Jesus identified Himself as the Cornerstone,

applying Psalm 118:22 to Himself, why did that take courage? How does Luke 20 encourage us to be boldly evangelistic?

2. STRONG TEACHING

"built on the foundation of the apostles and prophets, Christ Jesus himself being the cornerstone" (Ephesians 2:20)

A prominent evangelical pastor, who I still like very much, really threw his former family under the bus. Speaking to a group of Facebook employees, he told why he left his old church. "According to the Bible, every single one of these people has a supernatural gift that's meant to be used for the body. And I'm like 5,000 people show up every week to hear my gift, see my gift. That's a lot of waste…We're a body. I'm one member, maybe I'm the mouth. But if the mouth is the only thing that's working and…I'm trying to drag the rest of the body along, chewing on the carpet…" We see where the pastor was going with this.

Notwithstanding the inappropriateness of the venue he chose for voicing his frustrations with the way things were, I question the assumptions that undergird his complaint. I'm going to share why, because it cuts to the heart of a misunderstanding that many evangelicals have today.

The pastor's criticism can only be valid if the act of listening to a sermon is a passive thing. But if you think that on Sunday mornings, one man uses his spiritual gift while an audience of potential-filled believers sits idly by, then you are missing the very point of what a sermon is.

Listening to a sermon is not a passive thing. It is just as active as preaching one. If the listener is blessed to have in the pulpit a very good expositor (what I hope to be one day), then listening to the sermon is akin to eating a meal. It requires attention to what you are doing, as well as effort to chew and swallow the food. You should pray for God to bless the meal for the nourishment of the body. And hopefully, the whole experience is enjoyable. But it is not passive.

If the preacher is prone to miss the intent of the Author whose Word he is presenting, then the listener must be especially active as the food gets delivered to the table. The worse the preacher is at expositing, the more the listener has to do. Like an engine on overdrive, the mind should be revved up and alert, constantly correlating what the preacher says to other passages that come to mind (Acts 17:11) and comparing the preacher's exposition with the plain meaning of the text at hand.

But whether you have a good preacher, who sets the table and all you have to do is eat, or a bad one, who ought to go back to seminary to learn what exegesis is, the listeners' role is never passive. The sermon is the God-ordained meal for the sheep. It's been served every Sunday morning for 2,000 years for a reason. Actively listening to it transforms the believer into the image of Christ. Or, to return to our Cornerstone analogy, the sermon is foundational to the structure of the Church, which exists to uphold the truth. The Church is "a pillar and buttress of the truth" (1 Timothy 3:15).

We turn to Pastor Bob Spicer to help us understand the importance of Expository Bible Preaching .

Pastor Bob Spicer, Grace Bible Church

<u>Defining Expository Bible Preaching</u>

In order to meaningfully defend the importance of expository preaching, I need to make sure that what I mean by that term is clear. By it I mean preaching through a passage in such a way as <u>first</u> to draw out what the text meant to the original recipients and <u>then</u> what it means to us today. In order to do that, I need to do a historical, grammatical, contextual study of the passage. Usually, that will mean working my way through entire books of the Bible, paragraph by paragraph.

In the following paragraphs, I hope to demonstrate why I believe this kind of preaching ought to be the predominant method of feeding God's people in the church.

Philosophical/Theological Reasons

If God's people are to read the Bible intelligently so that they can understand and apply it to their lives, they need to know several things about it that, I am convinced, can best be taught by expository preaching. For example, they need to know the storyline of the Bible, so they can understand how the whole fits together.

In my early years as a child growing up in a Christian home, going to good evangelical churches (just about every time the door was opened), memorizing Bible verses, my perception of the Bible was that it was a collection of miscellaneous verses that supported what my church and my family believed.

Perhaps more than anything else, the Bible's storyline helps us to see how sin entered the world, and how God has worked to remedy that situation, and how He will ultimately deal with it. Preaching through the historical books of the Bible is the best way I can think of to do that.

People also need to know the different genres of material in the Bible, and how to read and apply them, so as to profit from them the best way they can. I will give only two examples. The wisdom literature of the Bible needs to be read differently from other genres. For example, there is a difference between a proverb and a promise. A proverb is just that, a wise saying that is nearly always true. Proverbs 10:27 reads, *"The fear of the Lord prolongs life, but the years of the wicked will be short."* Is that <u>always</u> true? It is certainly wise counsel, but it is not always how life works. Proverbs 22:6 reads, *"Train up a child in the way he should go; even when he is old he will not depart from it."* Are there not some children of very godly parents who have gone astray? Still, it is good counsel to train up our children in the way they should go.

Ecclesiastes is another example of wisdom literature that must be read a bit differently. If I rightly understand the point of the book, the writer is saying that if we live life only or primarily for what is temporal (under the sun), life will be vain, futile, to no purpose. If we live life in the material realm (under the sun) enjoying God's good gifts while living for eternal purposes, our lives can have meaning and fulfillment and purpose.

I believe that people learn most effectively how to read, interpret and apply the various genres of material in the Bible as they sit under expository preaching through those sections. Someone might argue that people can be taught principles of hermeneutics, for example, in a Sunday School class. But I would respond that a much more effective way is for them to see by example how the different kinds of material ought to be treated.

Still another reason why I am convinced that expository preaching ought to be the "meat and potatoes" of preaching is that God's people need to develop a Biblically based worldview. It is certainly possible that a series on marriage or on finances or on child rearing or on anger or on lust or on the use of the tongue may all be helpful to God's people in dealing with those particular issues. However, those same issues would be addressed as one preaches though the whole Bible. Furthermore, topical preaching alone may address specific issues well but it will not equip them to have a Biblical worldview. I am convinced that expository preaching will accomplish the same goals while showing how dealing with those issues flows out of a complete understanding of the way God wants us to look at all of life.

Textual Reasons

Another reason why I believe in the importance of expository preaching is that the claims the Bible makes for itself would seem to require it. For example, we who are evangelical Christians rightly place great emphasis on 2 Timothy 3:16-17: "*All Scripture is breathed out by God and profitable for teaching, for reproof, for correction, and for training in righteousness, that the*

man of God may be complete, equipped for every good work."
To support our belief in verbal, plenary inspiration we observe that the text says, All Scripture is God breathed. If we really believe that statement, how can we not preach the whole Bible, including the texts which are difficult? The sentence goes on to say that the same subject (all Scripture) is *"profitable for teaching, for reproof, for correction, and for training in righteousness, that the man of God may be complete, equipped for every good work."* If God says that the entire Bible is profitable, then it is. If God says that His design for giving us all of Scripture is so that we can be complete, equipped for every good work, then if we wish to be so equipped, we need to study all of it.

If we do not do so, the only logical conclusion I can come to is that to some degree and in some measure, we will be unequipped to do what He wants us to do. I realize that some texts are more readily applicable than others. It is easier to see the moral/spiritual applications of some texts than it is for others. Still, if I really believe what 2 Timothy says, then I am not in a position to omit passages from the Bible from my teaching.

My responsibility is to seek the help of the Holy Spirit to discern why He placed those passages in the Bible, and then try to understand what truths are there and how He would like for me to apply them to God's people. This position does not mean that I will spend an equal amount of time on every passage, but it will mean that I will not omit any of it in my teaching. It does not mean that every text is suitable for every audience, but all of it should be suitable for some. It does not mean that I will cover every passage in the same way, but in some manner I will seek to cover all of it.

Personal Reasons

Before I begin I would like to admit that this section is very subjective. That does not necessarily mean it is wrong, however. I believe I came to saving faith in Jesus one Sunday night in the Arlington Street Baptist Church in Akron, Ohio when I was about 7 ½ years old. At the conclusion of the sermon, I responded to the altar call, was led to faith by a counselor, and was baptized not long thereafter.

For many years I struggled with a lack of assurance of my salvation. During those years my family regularly attended good Gospel-preaching churches where Bible-based topical preaching was the norm. For me, the Bible became a collection of miscellaneous proof texts to support the positions my family and my church took on various theological issues. Most of my growing up years we attended church Sunday morning for Sunday School, Morning Worship, Evening Worship, and Wednesday nights, VBS, and in high school, youth group and Christian Service Brigade. I even taught a Sunday School class of little children for a while. Still I lacked assurance of my salvation. After finishing high school, I was able to enroll in what was then LeTourneau College (now University). I took the required courses in Old and New Testament Survey and then some courses in Biblical content. I began to see the story line of the Bible and how it fits together. I saw the different kinds of material that were in it and how to read those genres. I saw that salvation is all of God.

Then, one day, I noticed that I no longer doubted my salvation. I had assurance that I was a child of God. I believe that change occurred because I saw the Bible as a whole and from that began to develop a Christian worldview. I decided that what my teachers had done for me, I wanted to do for others for the rest of my life. I wanted to become a Bible expositor. For over forty years, I have endeavored to practice expository preaching, and it has been the joy of my life.

Thank you, Pastor Bob, for your encouraging words.

Cornerstone Strong—Ephesians 2

The book of Ephesians is about the Church. Ephesians begins with the Trinity creating the body, with Christ as our head and filling us "all in all" (Ephesians 1). It reminds us of our previous deadness in sin (2:1-3) and the glorious imposition of grace, whereby God in His mercy steps in to save us, entirely of His own doing, rendering us non-contributors, simply His workmanship (2:4-10).

Chapter 2, verse 11 reminds us that Ephesus is a Gentile town, so the Church there was mostly made up of Gentiles, just as most of us are, living in America. Yet, although we were without "hope and without God in the world" (2:12), we "have been brought near by the blood of Christ" (2:13). Gentile believers, no longer alienated from God, but together with believing Jews, are part of this new thing called "the Church", which is the household of God (2:14-19). That's the context of our next "Cornerstone" passage.

"So then you are no longer strangers and aliens, but you are fellow citizens with the saints and members of the household of God, built on the foundation of the apostles and prophets, Christ Jesus himself being the Cornerstone" (Ephesians 2:19-20).

The Person of Christ is the cornerstone that anchors and gives rise to the Church. But the rest of the building's foundation—the Church's concrete floor—is "the foundation of the apostles and prophets". In this context, "apostles" oversee the establishment of the Church, and by virtue of putting God's message to the Church (and to the world) *in writing*, they oversee the composition of the New Testament. Correspondingly, the term "prophets" stands as a metonym for the entire Old Testament, from Genesis, written by the prophet Moses, to Malachi's testimony, the last of the prophets' books handed down to us before the prophets fell silent for 400 years. So, according to Ephesians, the Church is built on Jesus as the Cornerstone, with the 66 books of the Bible completing the foundation. Who, then, are we—the Church—to be, given that we are built upon these 66 books?

Exegetes

In koine Greek, the prefix "ek", which transliterates to the English as "ex", means "out from". An exegete is one who draws *out from* the text the meaning that is resident there. By contrast, an *eisegete* reads *into* the text a meaning that he wants to find there (and, by the way, in my experience, "eisegete" also serves well as a nickname that seminary students use to make fun of each other). We don't want to be eisegetes. We want to exegete the Scriptures.

The most important place where exegesis needs to take place is in the pastor's study. Before ever taking to the pulpit, he must spend many hours with the text he plans to preach, making sure he understands what the Author is saying. The Sunday morning sermon has for 2,000 years, and especially since the Reformation began in 1517, taken up a majority of the service time on the Lord's Day. And it is entirely appropriate that it be this way, because the Cornerstone founds His Church upon the apostles and prophets. So, to devote an hour or so to the hearing of the Word is not bothersome or lamentable (as many evangelicals unfortunately veer off into believing), but is *foundational*, by definition.

The second most important place where exegesis needs to take place is the private study of every teacher in the church. Whether preparing for Children's Church—which is especially important if that time stands in place of the Sunday morning sermon for the very young—or a small group, an adult Sunday School, a devotional at a men's or women's event, or any other place where the Word will be taught, the teacher must study carefully, rightly dividing the Word (2 Timothy 2:15).

Finally, another highly important place where exegesis needs to take place is wherever any believer sits to read the Bible. Private devotions ought not be like reaching into a grab-bag, fishing for a verse that will tell me what I am trying to hear. Rather, we must approach the text humbly and prayerfully, and studiously seek the meaning of any passage that we read from the surrounding context. Always seek to understand what the Author intended, never what you want to hear Him say.

Expositors

Exegesis (drawing out the meaning already in the text) should happen in the study, but exposition happens in some context of the church. The Pastor preaching on Sunday and the Teacher teaching in various church contexts would be remiss if they stopped at the point of having exegeted the text. They may understand the text well enough, but their job is to explain the meaning, to lay it out before other people. From the crusade preacher standing before 10,000 to the mom teaching her child at night-night, all Christians should be growing as expositors of the Bible. We have no other foundation on which to build.

Let's define "exposit". The prefix "ex" followed by what it is you "posit"—what you *argue* or *explain*—renders *to explain out of*. Expositors explain out of the text the meaning we find there. We hold the book up, with all reverence, and give *the sense of it* to those who will listen.

"And Ezra opened the book in the sight of all the people, for he was above all the people, and as he opened it, all the people stood. And Ezra blessed the Lord, the great God, and all the people answered, 'Amen, Amen,' lifting up their hands. And they bowed their heads and worshipped the Lord with their faces to the ground. Also [some expositors] helped the people to understand the Law, while the people remained in their places. They read from the book, from the Law of God, clearly, and they gave the sense, so that the people understood the reading" (Nehemiah 8:5-8, interjection mine).

Herein, Nehemiah gives us *the sense* of what it means to preach or teach expositorily. I can't add anything to it. Our job, under the New Covenant, is to exposit both the Old and the New, to give the sense of the apostles and prophets, so that the people understand the reading.

Extremists

A final "ex" is called for, with regard to our handling of the Scriptures. An online dictionary defines an "extreme" as something that is "the furthest from the center or a given point; the uttermost". Our approach to the Bible needs to be as far *out from* the center as possible. Our secular humanist culture has no problem with the Bible, so long as you hold it as close to your heart as possible and keep yourself in the center. If you start with the presuppositions of postmodernism—that no truth is absolute, that all truth is subjective to the person who holds the belief—then the culture will bless your heart and approve of your private religion.

However, if you are an extremist, and hold the Bible out away from yourself, as a standard that is not only true for yourself but objectively true for all people, then the culture will tar and feather you. But, like followers of the Way, who were taunted by the name "Christian" until they turned around and embraced it, or like the Bible Thumping Wingnut, who was taunted for His preaching until he turned around and started an amazing podcast by that derogatory name, we need to embrace being labeled "extremists".

We are extremists. We are as far away from the cultural center as possible. They hold humanity at the center as the final arbiter of truth. All truth is subjective to individuals. The individual has absolute autonomy to hold any interpretation of the Bible that feels right. But we hold God at the center. He holds out His Word to us as the final arbiter of truth. All truth is objective, because it is defined by Him. He reveals truth to us in His Word, which we are not free to distort to fit our private opinions, but which stands unassailably as judge over us. We hold the culturally extreme view that God has spoken, that He spoke with clarity, and that we are mere creatures under His authority.

Extremists don't just listen to the Word once a week, on Sunday morning. Extremists eat the Word for breakfast, lunch, and dinner. Extremists can't stop talking about the Word. Extremists never tire of hearing the Word. Extremists can't stomach eisegesis. Extremists are exegetes and expositors who never say enough.

Application

Under the weight of much cultural pressure to abandon the clear teachings of the Bible, a thriving church will be one that remains thoroughly Biblical. As the surrounding culture drives off the cliff, self-destructing in its secular humanism, strong churches—pillars and supports of the truth—will stand strong upon the apostles and prophets. From that firm foundation, we will hold forth the truth to all who seek refuge from the storm. The structures of our culture are built on sinking sand. But we stand upon the Word. Hold it fast without compromise (Philippians 2:16).

Moreover, it is incumbent upon every Christian, not just the minister, to become a true student of the Word. Learn to be an exegete, paying special attention—actively listening—to the sermon every Sunday morning. Do so with the eagerness that comes from understanding that you are also called to exposit the Scriptures. Whether your audience will be one child in a passing encounter or a congregation on the Lord's Day, prepare to exposit the Scriptures like one who will have to give an account to the Author of the book you set out to explain. Tremble at the responsibility.

"But this is the one to whom I will look: he who is humble and contrite in spirit and trembles at my word" (Isaiah 66:2b).

Tremble, but do not be paralyzed. Remember our commissioning (Matthew 28:18-20). Until Christ returns, we are to be about the business of making disciples. And if Jesus was so extreme as to shed His blood to make disciples, so, likewise, ought we become extremists. If we want to be strong members of a thriving church—strong enough to overcome the world, then we're going to need to let go of many of our worldly pursuits. Replace those things with daily study of the Word. Learn to be an exegete, and an expositor, and an extremist. Thriving churches are built with strong teaching.

Discussion Questions

What was the misunderstanding that led the prominent pastor to think that he was doing all the work on Sunday mornings while the congregation was passive?

What do you and your church need to learn from what Pastor Bob had to say?

What is the role of the listener when a sermon is being preached? How active is your mind during the Sunday morning hour?

What is the difference between exegesis and eisegesis? Why is it so important to become a good exegete?

What does Nehemiah 8 teach us about becoming an expositor? Who needs to be good at exposition?

If allowed to observe all your Bible study time, would an unbeliever describe you as an extremist?

Why is the culture OK with Christians holding private beliefs in the Bible but not OK with Christians holding those beliefs as absolute truth?

What views do you hold, on account of biblical exegesis, that most people in America would consider extreme? How does being considered an extremist affect you?

How important is it to have expository preaching, rather than topical sermons, in the Sunday morning worship service?

3. STRONG THEOLOGY

"This Jesus is the stone that was rejected by you, the builders, which has become the cornerstone" (Acts 4:11)

"to do whatever your hand and your plan had predestined to take place" (Acts 4:28)

Where I attended seminary, there are two separate departments devoted to teaching the Bible. For about 30 credit hours, the Bible Exposition Department takes you through the 66 books of the Bible, chapter by chapter, verse by verse. For another 30 credit hours, the Systematic Theology Department takes you through the major areas of theology (Trinitarianism, Soteriology, Ecclesiology, etc.).

Like mowing a lawn in two directions to create a checkered pattern, the departments cover the same turf, but from different angles. Bible Ex. is foundational, because we allow the apostles and prophets to speak for themselves. But S.T. courses matter too, because they allow the entirety of the Bible to speak to any given topic, protecting us from misinterpretations at any given verse. Biblical exposition is paramount, but, as both Albert Mohler and James White like to say, "theology matters".

Churches with strong theology are like boats with enough ballast to keep from tipping when the seas get rough. Build a church on the personality of a dynamic pastor and people will come, at least until he leaves. Build a church on the emotions of high energy music and people will come, at least until they get bored even with that. Build a church on signs and wonders, or the pursuit of the "presence of God", as if He's not here with us all the time, and people will come until the man of God with "an even stronger anointing" moves into town. Build a church on strong theology and it will withstand the test of time.

The only churches with robust theology that I have ever seen fail are those that departed from the very theological roots that made them strong in the first place. Witness the many mainline churches in America, born of the Reformation cry "sola scriptura!", now denying biblical inerrancy and bleeding members year by year.

Strong theology won't create a flood of new people pouring through the front door of the church. But, over time, as regular attenders develop their systematic theology, strong theology will close the back door. The key is to be *always reforming* ("semper reformanda"), never thinking that we have everything figured out, but always looking to God in the Scriptures, asking Him to conform our worldview to His.

Developing a strong systematic theology is like loading biblical data into the library that is your brain, which has a card catalog of sorts (do libraries still have those?). As we encounter truths in God's Word, we file them away into appropriate categories, labeling as we go. When questions arise, if they have some theological bearing, we find the card that applies, then open the section of our brain that holds the appropriate parts of Scripture.

As we constantly add to our theological knowledge bank, it becomes rich with Scriptural truth. As a result, our decision making becomes increasingly pleasing to God. Churches that grow strong in theology will please God, and He will make them thrive.

We look to Pastor Warren Boettcher for words of exhortation as to why "theology matters" in the life of the church.

Pastor Warren Boettcher, Sovereign Grace Church

Why Doctrine Matters!

Doctrine. A small word filled with great power. A word that can be marked with confusion, if not dread, and a word that can take an amicable discussion and turn it into a heated debated. Why doctrine? Hasn't it been the source of division within the Christian church? Wouldn't we all be better off just simply "loving Jesus"? Or perhaps we could give a nod and admit that doctrine is important to trained theologians, but not so much for the average person just trying to pay their bills and care for their family. Those in the "ivory towers" of learning might love to study and discuss, but it's not of much use to those of us "slugging it out in the trenches".

While perhaps just "loving Jesus" seems attractive to us at first glance, the moment we even begin to ask any type of serious question about God or life or suffering, we begin to realize that ignoring doctrine is an inadequate answer. After all, I could say "I love Jesus" and have no clue as to who He *really* is, what He has *really* done, or what He *really* requires of me. Questions like: who is God and what is He like; why am I here; and what will happen when I die, are all questions of doctrine. We all think about these types of questions at some point in our lives. Therefore, everyone has doctrine; the only question is if it is Biblically sound or not.

Here's the crux of the matter: Sound Doctrine is foundational to Christian discipleship (following Jesus) and Christian experience (enjoying Jesus). Theologian Sinclair Ferguson captures this well when he writes, "The conviction that Christian doctrine matters for Christian living is one of the most important growth points for Christian life." So, if sound doctrine is that important for Christian living, the devaluing of doctrine is that dangerous. Albert Mohler, President of Southern Baptist Theological Seminary, insightfully comments that; "Those who sow disdain and disinterest in biblical doctrine will reap a harvest of rootless and fruitless Christians. Churches lacking an intentional and effective program of doctrinal instruction risk becoming the company of the confused…The low state of doctrinal understanding among so many evangelicals is evidence of a profound failure of both nerve and conviction. Both must be recovered if there is to be anything even remotely *evangelical* about evangelicalism of the future."

However, the most powerful argument for sound doctrine comes from the Bible itself. In I Timothy 1, Paul instructs Timothy to charge people "not to teach any different doctrine" (vs. 3), because certain people were coming up with new and clever ideas that promoted "speculations" (vs. 4), "vain discussions" (vs. 6), and "confident assertions" (vs. 7) that, in turn, were leading Christians astray and weakening the church. The American church seems to have the same susceptibility. How often do we hear about the latest key to happiness, or unlocking effective prayer, the hidden secret of world evangelization, the prophetic meaning of political events, or confident assertions about the date of the return of Christ? How often do American Christians chase the latest greatest idea or the next place of spiritual revival or ecstatic experience? May we hear Mohler's warning about being "rootless and fruitless" and thank God that He gives sound doctrine to protect us. May we hear Paul's instruction to Timothy, and God's instruction to us, that we teach nothing that "is contrary to sound doctrine, in accordance with the glorious gospel of the blessed God" (vs. 10-11). So, why sound doctrine?

First and foremost, it helps us know God accurately and love Him joyfully. It's by the Bible through the teaching of sound doctrine that we know God. Without this, we run into the temptation and danger of making God in our own image, which is the worst form of idolatry. Jesus says in John 4:23-24, "But the hour is coming, and is now here, when the true worshipers will worship the Father in spirit and truth, for the Father is seeking such people to worship him. God is spirit, and those that worship him must worship in spirit and truth." The Bible is God's great revelation of Himself and the great revelation of the story of redemption from beginning to end. Sound doctrine proclaims and protects both! There are people we meet that the more we get to know them the less impressive they become (I'm one of those people!). However, God is just the opposite, the more you get to know Him, the greater He is in your eyes and the more you love Him.

We would dishonor Him and impoverish ourselves if we neglected the sound doctrines that open our eyes to the glory of God. Words like sovereignty, immutability, faithfulness, holiness, justice, grace, aseity, eternity, omniscience, omnipotence, goodness, love, mercy, and glory are not just theological or doctrinal words to be understood, but amazing truths to be comforted by and enjoyed. Like anything meaningful and important, these are truths to be studied, and the effort put forth to do so is profoundly worthwhile and satisfying.

Second, it produces stability. Our culture is changing and changing so fast it makes one's head spin. How do we remain stable when everything around is changing and everything we believe is being challenged? Sound doctrine becomes an unshakeable rock! Paul writes in Ephesians 4:13-14, "so that we may no longer be children, tossed to and fro by the waves and carried about by every wind of doctrine, by human cunning, by craftiness in deceitful schemes. Rather, speaking the truth in love, we are to grow up in every way into him who is the head, into Christ." When Scripture refers to "the truth", we should see that not as our feelings or opinions about something, but as the exposition (speaking) of the Gospel with all its blessings, promises, and claims into one another's lives, motivated by love for that person. Without this sound doctrine, we are prey to be "tossed to and fro...and carried about by every wind of doctrine", with the possibility of losing our footing amongst life's challenges.

Sound doctrine protects us and brings us stability through discernment, and we must remember that false doctrine can often be subtle in its presentation. 19th Century preacher Charles Spurgeon said, "Discernment is not simply a matter of telling the difference between right and wrong; rather it is the difference between right and almost right." When culture changes, experts redefine right and wrong, and suffering comes; the knowledge of God through the truths of Scripture becomes a mighty refuge and fortress.

Finally, sound doctrine produces maturity. When we "speak the truth in love" we "grow up in every way into him who is the head, into Christ from whom the whole body, joined and held together by every joint with which it is equipped, when each part is working properly, makes the body grow so that it builds itself up in love" (Eph. 4:15-16). Sound doctrine produces maturity in the individual and in the church. It shows us how we are to live and what convictions should be moving us forward.

For example, why should we forgive in relationships? This is a common and often frustrating human experience. It exists in the trenches of normal everyday life and can be disabling. How does doctrine speak to us and produce real maturity? The world might give counsel that says, 'the person you don't forgive has power over you or that you need to forgive for your own mental and emotional health'. Sound doctrine blows that out of the water as a shallow and powerless response. We forgive because God has forgiven us (Ephesians 4:32; see Matthew

18:21-35 for a great exposition of this truth). Sound doctrine moves forgiveness from a purely horizontal human interaction to a God-centered grace-empowered interaction that reflects a growing maturity in the Christian's life. Of course I don't treat others as they may deserve, because God has not treated me that way. I understand that God loved me when I was completely unlovely and therefore I can love someone else who is a tad "messy".

The truths of sound doctrine will produce a maturity that forgives others well and loves them well. The truths about God, the cross, and His grace and mercy towards our sinfulness (all sound doctrine points) will produce maturity. Maturity not marked by any self-righteousness or theological superiority, but marked by a deep humility that stands in amazement of a great Savior and a joyful trust in our great God!

Thank you, Pastor Warren, for your encouraging words.

Cornerstone Strong—Acts 4

Acts 4:1 finds two apostles boldly preaching the gospel in the Temple and the leaders of the Temple very upset about it. The number of believers grows to 5,000 and the apostles wind up in jail (4:2-4). The next day, the leaders question the apostles. Peter, speaking for the other, attributes the healing of the cripple (which is what drew the crowd in the Temple in the first place) to the matchless name of Jesus

Christ of Nazareth (4:5-10). Then, evidently not in the least bit afraid of the leaders, Peter says,

"This Jesus is the stone that was rejected by you, the builders, which has become the cornerstone" (Acts 4:11).

Peter is not one to pull any punches. He goes on to proclaim the exclusivity of salvation. Jesus is now risen from the dead, so it is *only* the name of Jesus by which *anyone* will be saved (4:12). The Temple leaders were shocked by Peter's boldness (4:13) and silenced by the evidence of a former cripple now healed and standing in their midst (4:14). So, they took a private moment to deliberate (4:15-17). Then they reconvened with Peter and John and commanded them not to speak any more in the name of Jesus (4:18).

At that, Peter and John are both so quick to speak that our text gives their answer as a conglomeration of their two voices. "But Peter and John answered them" (4:19), and what they said was bold and defiant. They assured the leaders that they would obey God, not them (4:19-20). To which, we would expect the leaders to initiate another round of crucifixions. But no, providence will not allow it. Because so many people witnessed the healing, because they are now watching what the leaders will do, the leaders are hamstrung. God providentially uses the force of public opinion to prevent the evil intentions of the leaders (4:21-22), and the apostles are released (4:23).

Peter and John immediately return to their own, a much friendlier crowd, and the whole lot of them turn to the Lord in prayer. The substance of their prayer is providentially preserved for us. First, they confess God's absolute sovereignty (4:24)—that the Creator of all things is absolutely in control of all things He created. Second, they process the events of their present experience through the lens of the Word of God, quoting from Psalm 2:1-2 and recognizing the vanity of any human effort to take anything away from the sovereignty of God (4:25-26). Third, they recognize that 4 distinct entities, all with sinful intentions of their own, all operating according to their own creaturely willfulness, worked together to do the most heinous thing ever to happen on the face of the earth. The crucifixion of the precious Lamb of God was their doing. Nevertheless, they pray these massively important words—words that ought to transform our theology. The 4 entities (Herod, Pilate, Gentiles, Israelites) were *only* able "to do whatever your hand and your plan had predestined to take place" (4:28).

Acts 4 rounds out with an appeal to God for even more boldness in preaching the gospel than the apostles have demonstrated thus far, which was already pretty good (4:29-31)! We also get a glimpse of the tremendous generosity that characterized this group of young believers (4:32-37). But the thrust of Acts 4 must not be missed. God is sovereign. His providence controls everything that happens under the sun. Therefore, we Christians have no need to fear anything. Our theological knowledge of His predestination (Acts 4:28), if we couple that knowledge with petitions for boldness (Acts 4:29), enables us to be as bold as lions (Proverbs 28:1). We are called to be Calvinistic Compatibilistic confident Christians.

Calvinistic

Calvinism is not a dirty word. And it doesn't imply devotion to the Frenchman, John Calvin. After Luther, John Calvin was probably the foremost leader of the Protestant Reformation, but he was never trying to get his name on the thing.

The system of theology known today as Calvinism received its name nearly 100 years after Calvin, once the Reformation began to splinter in so many directions that it became helpful to identify various streams by simple terms to represent each one. Thus, when Arminius challenged the orthodoxy of the Dutch reformed churches and, in 1618-1619, when a massive ecumenical council met in Dort to address his propositions, the followers of Arminius' way of thinking began to be called "Arminians" and the orthodoxy of the council (and of the vast majority of the first 100 years of the Reformation, except for the Lutherans who splintered off into their own unique brand of theology) came to be called

"Calvinism". To call oneself a "Calvinist" is simply to identify within that stream of theology, not to claim adherence to the man, nor even everything he believed and taught.

America has seen two "Great Awakenings", the first Calvinistic, the second Arminian. Most of our inherited theological tradition, most of what identifies as "evangelical" in America today, is far more influenced by the latter—Arminianism (John Wesley was the foremost proponent to popularize it).

But, as we have seen, Acts 4 presents a Calvinistic theological worldview. The fundamental difference between the two systems is the answer to the question, "whose will is ultimately free—God's or man's?" Arminians assert that, at some point, God is bound to abide by the final decision of people to either accept or reject Christ, since He has given everyone "free will". Calvinists agree that all people have a will, but assert that the will is only creaturely (not autonomous) and that it is actually bound (not free) until God mercifully grants repentance and faith to the person (2 Timothy 2:25), because God is the only Being in the universe who is ultimately free (Daniel 4:35).

At the outset of the Reformation, Luther represented the "Calvinistic" position, writing "The Bondage of the Will", while the Roman Catholic Desiderius Erasmus took the "Arminian" position, writing "The Freedom of the Will". Since Calvin and Arminius came later, it is anachronistic to speak of

Luther and Erasmus as a Calvinist and an Arminian, but the issue of ultimate freedom that launched the Reformation (Luther described the ultimate freedom issue as the hinge upon which the Reformation turned) really was the fundamental divide. Ironically, today, Evangelical churches in America are fundamentally divided between the same two theological schools of thought that started the Reformation in the first place—Calvinism and Arminianism.

Either the proposition of Calvinism (monergism—that one force, namely God's power, accomplishes salvation, not needing the cooperation of man) is true, or it is not true. The Calvinistic system of theology asserts that it is true, roundly proving that claim by 5 biblical propositions that fit together, each one making Calvinism the necessary conclusion, each one supported by concrete biblical exegesis. 1) People are totally unable to choose God (Romans 1:18-32, Ephesians 2:1, Romans 8:7-8). 2) God unconditionally chooses to save whom He will (Ephesians 1:3-14, Romans 9). 3) Jesus died and rose to actually save (not just make savable) a particular people (John 10:11, Ephesians 5:2, John 17:9, Titus 2:14). 4) Those whom God draws will, of a certainty, come to Christ at their appointed time (John 6:44, John 6:65, Ephesians 1:11-14). 5) Those whom God saves, He also keeps forever, such that we cannot be lost. True freedom is having nothing in the creaturely will that might (or could) ever leave Christ (Ephesians

1:14, Jude 24-25).

We return now to Acts 4 to seal the deal. If even the most heinous, most sinful, most evil human action in the history of the world was done according to God's free will, then how much more should we recognize that the glorious, happy, good act of God in saving sinners is according to God's free will? In sin, 4 groups conspired "to do whatever your hand and your plan had predestined to take place" (Acts 4:28). Notwithstanding the will of mere creatures, *God saves sinners according to what His hand and His plan predestines to take place*. Strong theology is Calvinistic.

Compatibilistic

The Bible presents us with a God who works out His plan in history, but people are not presented as being robotic. Rather, people are made in the image of God, which means, in part, that each of us has a will. People exercise their will according to what they desire most. Trouble is, affections are perverted by the fall of Adam, our earthly father. His nature became sinful when he rebelled in the Garden, and we inherited that sin nature from him. Therefore, although God is sovereign over all, the Bible presents us, not Him, as being responsible for sin. According to the Scriptures, human responsibility, as well as the human ability to make real choices, *is compatible* with a God who predestines, according to the Scriptures.

Acts 4 teaches this Compatibilism as clearly as anywhere else in the Bible. Pontius Pilate made a real choice, according to his own desires, to wash his hands of the travesty unfolding before his eyes. Herod the Tetrarch entertained himself by mocking the Messiah before handing him over to die. The Jews yelled "crucify!" from the seat of their deepest passions, from the depths of their hearts. The Romans carried out orders, content to get a paycheck. All 4 entities exercised their own wills. It was them who did it. They were responsible, and God was righteous to hold them responsible. They weren't robots. They were creatures making willful choices. *And what they did was predestined (Acts 4:28).*

We see the same thing in Genesis 50:20. What the brothers had meant for evil, God meant for good. God didn't just make good out of a bad situation. He *meant* the situation. We see the same in Isaiah 10. What the Assyrian King did in the haughtiness of his heart, God foreordained for the judgment of His people. It's all throughout the Bible. All the events of this world are predestined, but it is not a strict determinism. It is a soft determinism, whereby human responsibility is compatible with divine sovereignty.

Repenting of sin and believing in Christ is something that *you* do. "Having purified your souls by *your obedience* to the truth…" (1 Peter 1:22) implies that *you* actively do the repenting and believing. Nevertheless, it is also true that your creaturely will *will not* do it, for it is not even able to do so (Romans

8:7-8, Ephesians 2:1). For us who have repented and believed, it is grace alone that has proven sufficient to "cause us to be born again" (1 Peter 1:3). By this miracle of regeneration, our creaturely will gladly chooses to repent and believe. In our experience, it is we who do the repenting and believing. But it is God who does the saving. Our real choice to come to Christ is compatible with His sovereign choice that we would come. We preserve the reality of human choices, even as all glory goes to God, when our Calvinism is Compatibilistic.

Confident

Here's why this matters so much. The Biblical reasons above are why White and Mohler are right about their Calvinism, but in my opinion, the biggest reason they are right to say "theology matters" is because Calvinistic theology produces *confidence in God.*

I've preached too many funerals, mourned the loss of too many kids I loved, seen too many tragedies in the city, felt too much pain in watching loved ones suffer, to be anything but a Calvinist. Arminianism can offer me the hope that God is still in control to a certain degree. But at some point, according to their conception, God is sometimes bound by human free will (to say that "He ordained free will to determine some things" doesn't solve the problem that comes with libertarian free will—namely, that God now lacks control, at least to some degree). God can still work out a great plan, but only like a chess player. I need a hope that's bigger than that. The Calvinistic understanding is of a God who has a plan and a purpose for everything, including suffering. He doesn't *just* work everything out for good. His good plan includes the bad thing (Isaiah 45:7). The bad thing has a purpose. Everything will work together for the good of us who love Him (Romans 8:28) *because* He has ordained whatsoever comes to pass, and nothing—absolutely nothing—can frustrate His plan. The Christian who gets this will not be easily shaken.

Churches built on strong theology like this will not crumble under the weight of pressure. When financial budgets are not being met, when leading members move to a new city (or a new church in your same city), when differences of opinion raise the emotional temperature, when a thousand little things add up, strong Calvinists do not freak out! We'll bleed like anyone else. We'll mourn when it's time to mourn. But the peace that passes understanding is the peace that understands Who it is that's in control. Calvinistic churches trust that God has a purpose for the trials that come, so their confidence in God is not shaken by circumstance.

A non-Calvinist friend of mine likes to rib me about me being a "6-point Calvinist" (and I like to agree to the 6th point, whatever it is). He sometimes jokes that I don't have to worry about a certain sad thing that is likely to happen soon, because, says he, "you're a Calvinist, so if it happens, it is ordained to happen anyway". To that, I say "amen".

Peter and John, "filled with the Holy Spirit" (Acts 4:8), spoke to the Temple leaders, not like children freaking out over a game they're playing, but like men who are strong in their confidence in God (1 Corinthians 16:13). Peter and John trusted God's providence, and God's providence made a way for them to emerge unscathed from the murderous intentions of the very men who killed Jesus (Acts 4:19-22). Peter and John, bold as lions because they believed in providence (4:28), still prayed for more boldness (4:29-31), because bold confidence should be the posture of every child of God. God is in charge, so we are confident.

Application

If Calvinism has always been a dirty word to you, it is probably because the Arminian traditions of our culture, of which you may or may not be aware, have painted Calvinism in a derogatory light. It is often caricatured as a cold mechanical determinism, God at the strings, people jumping around like puppets. But the Bible tells the story of warm-blooded people making real choices for which they are responsible. The problem is not that they are being controlled. Their red-eyed passion fuels their sinful choices, and if offered the opportunity to come to Christ, their affection for sin would scorn the offer. Humans are responsible. Human responsibility is compatible with a free God, who sometimes leaves sinners in their wild-eyed hell-bound state and sometimes mercies other sinners with His unmerited gift of salvation. Sometimes He displays His justice. Other times, He displays His mercy. He is free to choose (Romans 9:18).

Believe it or not, God remains free. Wisdom beckons us to believe it and thus become a Calvinist. But even if not now, one day we Christians surely will believe it, when we are completely free in heaven (free of a nature that has any possibility of choosing sin in any way, shape, or form).

The same people who confessed predestination (Acts 4:28) prayed fervently for certain things they wanted God to do for them (4:29-31). That sounds like their practice contradicted their theology. But what we experience in this life, ordered as things are by laws of nature, by choices we make, and even by God's response to our prayers, is compatible with God having a sovereign decree before the foundation of the world. Our choices are compatible with His decree. So, pray for the things you need. Ask, first of all, for more boldness to preach the gospel. Don't rest sleepily in predestination (Peter and John didn't), but let your confident knowledge that God has a decree only fuel the fervency with which you pray. Ask for even more confidence to trust the Sovereign God.

Discussion Questions

If you were to go to seminary, what would be the difference between your Systematic Theology classes and Bible Exposition classes? Are both necessary? Is theological study only for pastors and seminary types?

What do you and your church need to learn from what Pastor Warren had to say?

How is Systematic Theology different from Biblical Exposition? Why are both important?

What does Acts 4 teach about God's ability to build a people upon the Cornerstone (Acts 4:11), to save whosoever He will (4:12, 27-28)?

Are any of the 5 propositions of the Calvinistic system lacking biblical support?

Why is compatibilism (soft determinism) preferable to a strictly deterministic worldview? Where are two or three places in the Scriptures that teach compatibilism?

Why is Calvinism so important for having confidence in God? Is predestination only about salvation, or does it affect all areas of our worldview?

If God has predestined everything, what's the point of praying? Do you think it is pleasing to God when we pray for boldness (confidence in Him)? Pray now according to the pattern of Acts 4:29-31.

4. STRONG GIFTS

"Oh come, let us sing to the Lord; let us make a joyful noise to the rock of our salvation!" (Psalm 95:1).

More Muslims have abandoned Islam and embraced Christianity in the last 50 years than in all the previous 1350 years of Islam's existence. I can't prove that, but I have heard many say so, and the anecdotal evidence I have heard from so many different sources convinces me that it is true. And from what I have heard, from Nabeel Qureshi, Tom Doyle, Joe Carey and many other experts, most have come to Christ partially through a charismatic experience. A gifted evangelist, often a Christian apologist, presents the Gospel. But then the Muslim has a dream or vision that confirms the message they heard from the gifted evangelist. Conversion often follows these charismatic experiences. But we have to be careful.

Has not the charismatic movement given birth to more cults, heresies, and wild un-Christ-like behavior than any other stream of Christianity? In my estimation, it certainly has. The prosperity gospel, the disparaging of doctrinal discernment, ecumenism with sub-Christian religions, the pursuit of signs and wonders (rather than the pursuit of Christ), snake handling, fire tunnels, grave soaking, slaying in the Spirit, running the aisles, holy laughter, leg lengthening, gold dust, gold teeth, frenzied dancing, petroleum consumption, live rat consumption, pyramid scheming, weird hair and outrageous makeup are all the unwelcome and unholy guests of the worldwide charismatic movement.

We have to be careful with the charismatic movement, and careful not to lend unqualified support to it, lest we become partner with these things that do not glorify God.

I have a good friend who is willing to walk closer to the charismatic movement than I am willing to do. He is prominent in the movement. What I would say to him and to any born-again Christian who ministers with him at their charismatic conferences is that I love you, I count you as a brother or sister, but the theology you present is distorted and the methods you use have not been careful enough. Walter Martin went on TBN in the 1980s and rebuked Kenneth Copeland and others for their "little god" theology. Instead of receiving that rebuke, Paul Crouch, the founder of TBN, made "heresy hunters" the special victims of his ire, railing against them often. He diminished the importance of doctrine, and Benny Hinn and other TBN personalities jumped on board with equally strong words. I hear the same rhetoric from many prominent charismatics today. But it is important that true listening begin to take place, in both directions.

The fundamental point that I would like to press with these leaders is the very idea that "theology matters". Don't fall in line with the postmodern worldview of the secular humanists. Postmoderns diminish the importance of doctrine and magnify the importance of experience, emotion, and pragmatism. Your desire to reach the world for Christ is great. But the methods you choose to use arise from your theology, and some of those methods run contra the theology of the Bible. And I don't just mean *my theology*, as if the Bible had no objective theology to present, as if doctrinal disagreements can be settled by allowing each to hold his own theology as being subjectively true. Theology matters and the Scriptures are clear. Where we disagree, the problem is with us.

Here are some specific problem areas that need to be addressed: 1) slaying in the Spirit, 2) public tongues without interpretation, 3) women as pastors, 4) promises of prosperity, and 5) gospel partnership with charismatic Catholics. Each of these contradict sound Biblical theology (1 Corinthians 14:26-35, 1 Peter 4:12, Galatians 1:6-9, 3:10). The Scriptures are clearly opposed to these things, but there needs to be prolonged theological engagement to show it forth.

I am fully confident that my charismatic friend loves the Lord. We worshipped Him together when we were young. Since then, we never stopped serving Him. Both of us still worship Him today. I hope he will receive this exhortation. I offer it publicly because the teachers on TBN and at the conferences are teaching publicly. And I welcome being shown if I have erred. I genuinely welcome it, and I would not be surprised if there are errors in my theology that someone may point out. We should all be open to receiving criticism. I offer correctives, and I am open to receiving them. We talk about these things because we care about each other and the Church. That said, we move on to the larger point of this chapter.

I do not believe that the Bible teaches Cessationism. When I read church history, I think it is undeniable that the quantity of organic healings, overt miracles, and unmistakable signs and wonders fell off considerably after the days of the apostles. But were any of us there to prove they ceased? And where in the Bible does it say they did? Or that they would? To argue for Cessationism by appealing to church history is merely an appeal to experience. But charismatics say they are experiencing supernatural spiritual gifts today. So, if it is only "he said, she said", where is the force of the historical argument for Cessationism?

Don't form theology from experience. Theology is revealed in the Bible, no matter what anyone of us experiences.

But, there is nothing wrong with experiences per say. For my part, I'll share that my experiences have included what I think are spiritual gifts. On several occasions, I have *felt* a strong indication (had a very clear impression in my mind) that I needed to go to a very specific location to meet a certain person. When I went, I found that person at the precise location I envisioned and I shared the gospel, which turned out to be powerful in their lives.

Once, I felt led to leave the house where I stayed in Dallas to "meet Kenny" (whom I had only met once before, several months prior) "on the corner of Globe and Shiloh". As I arrived at that exact intersection, so did Kenny, riding up quickly on a bike. We spent the rest of the day talking about the Lord, and he prayed, calling on Christ in what appeared to me to be genuine repentance and faith.

Another time, the Lord directed me to leave a wedding to "go share the gospel with Mormons". I didn't know where to look for Mormons, but I found two Mormons right outside the hotel where the reception was to be. They were walking along the road, so I offered them a ride. I drove them to their Mormon picnic, which was weird, because I had attended (by invitation) a Mormon picnic the weekend before. We talked at length about the Gospel, then I left.

I think all of these experiences were charismatic, because a gift of evangelism operated in me and the result was increased opportunity for sharing the gospel. In the case of the Mormons, they did not come to the true Christ at that time, but the words God gave me in that picnic encounter were precise, and the Mormons were clearly shaken in their false religion. By the way, after sharing the gospel for about an hour, I made it back to the reception in time for the cake. It was quite a surreal experience.

In the city of Philadelphia, we also saw several things happen that, in my mind, should be described as charismatic. For five years in a row, the day of our big evangelistic festival was met with severe thunderstorms. One year, that included a tornado warning and a 100% chance of rain in the forecast. But our team prayed each time, believed that God would move the storm, and each time, the skies held back their rain for the 4 hours of the evangelistic festival. The year of the tornado warning, the first drop of rain fell at 5:59 pm, the festival ended at 6:00, and we welcomed all the people into our building to have a church service as a storm broke loose outside. We had prepared that indoor service at the end of the outdoor festival because of a dream I had several days before. When events unfolded, what I saw in the dream actually happened. What's more, the rain at the close of the festival drove all the people into the building to hear more of the gospel!

A very similar event unfolded for us a couple of years later at another church plant in a different part of Philadelphia. I think that the spiritual gift of the

Ephesians 4:11 evangelist and the 1 Corinthians 12:10 "working of miracles" operated each of those times, for the purpose of sharing the gospel, but I am not dogmatic about this claim. It's only my own personal experience. And all the glory for it belongs entirely to God. The gifts of the Spirit are only by His grace.

What I do want to teach is that the Bible is silent about the cessation of spiritual gifts at any point (death of the last apostle, completion of the canon) until Christ returns. We should, therefore, expect the spiritual gifts to operate, since commentary regarding their use is, in fact, found in 1 Corinthians 12-14, among other places (the lists of spiritual gifts are found in 1 Corinthians 12, Romans 12, 1 Peter 4, and Ephesians 4).

Additionally, it seems to me (here is an ancillary argument from experience…not the basis of theology but certainly helpful for undercutting Cessationist arguments based on church history) that the thriving churches of the world today are more often charismatic than not. The center of gravity for the growth of Christianity has shifted South and East. Subsaharan Africa, India, China, and South America are surpassing the North and West in numbers of Christians. In all these places, even more so than in North America, it is largely the charismatic churches that are thriving.

Likewise, charismatic churches are thriving in America today, especially in reaching the younger generation. I have already sounded a note of concern about charismatic churches in America, and Bethel Church in Redding, CA falls right there in that camp. But I'll use them to make the larger point of this chapter, having already stated my caveats. I have seen the Lord use Bethel Worship music in powerful ways, even building the faith of many as they battle with various afflictions. We should recognize that thousands of millennials passionately worshipping the Lord Jesus Christ is not the work of devils, even though any error belongs to devils, but is, by in large, the work of the Holy Spirit.

I would rather worship like the true believers at Bethel or Hillsong or the Jesus Conference than to sit arms folded in a cold heartless "worship service". Orthodoxy when it loses its first love becomes nothing more than a social club of the "frozen chosen". But it doesn't have to be either/or. We can have sound doctrine with passionate worship. And, by the way, a warm heart doesn't have to manifest in any outward mannerism. Worship is a matter of the heart. But when you see Christians kneeling before the Father (Psalm 95:6), tears running down their faces, voices belting out worship to the Lamb of God, it makes you want to jump right in. And I would argue...it is a good thing if you do.

We have to be careful, but I do think that we should be charismatic. Thriving churches are carefully Charismatic, having strong gifts.

Pastor Bill Luebkemann, Calvary Chapel of Marlton

Bill Luebkemann, like the other 4 guys who contributed to this book, is a perfect example of a spiritually gifted man who retains the spirit of the Luke 17:10 servant. I've talked with him a lot about writing this segment on how the spiritual gifts operated through him for the founding of Calvary Chapel of Marlton, the development of Joyful Noise Christian School, and the creation of Hope FM, which now broadcasts the Gospel 24 hours a day, 7 days a week, all across Maryland, Pennsylvania, and New Jersey. But, he pretty much shrugs his shoulders and displays little interest in telling the story of how he did it.

That's because Bill knows he didn't do it. Whatever has been accomplished has been the work of the Spirit of God. Since Bill believes, as I do, that the charismatic gifts are for today, and since this chapter of ours seeks to teach careful charismaticism to the body of Christ, he agreed to let me say what we have here.

When Bill became pastor, the church was part of a Baptist denomination. The church wasn't thriving at the time. In fact, it had dwindled down to only a few people when Bill stepped in to lead. In 1997, he led the church into the Calvary Chapel movement, which deserves some commentary at this point.

Much of the fruit that has come from Calvary Chapel is owed in part to the operation of spiritual gifts. First, Maranatha Music revolutionized Christian music. Today's Contemporary Christian Music, despite problems of its own, is a tremendous blessing to the Church, and much of it began with Calvary Chapel. Second, Calvary Chapel pushed expository bible preaching into the mainstream of American evangelicalism. That was a mighty work of the Spirit that needs to be celebrated. Third, Calvary Chapel bolstered evangelical support for the nation of Israel. Fourth, CC has reached hundreds of thousands of young people that other churches have largely failed to reach. Finally, the list could go on and on, since high schools, bible colleges, radio stations, and missionaries the world over have been ministering under the CC banner for years. All these mighty works continue on today, showing no sign of fading.

And that brings us back to Pastor Bill. Through the encouragement of Pastor Chuck Smith, through seasons of prayer with the Lord, through sensing God's leading, Bill has been used by God to build a Christian School and a network of radio stations, plus an app and website (without quitting his day job). The only explanation for how all that was possible is that the Spirit of God gifted Bill in his speaking, his leading, his planning, and his decision making. It was beyond natural ability. Bill exercised his spiritual gifts.

Hope FM has done more for the gospel than any of us know. As I look out on a Sunday morning I can count half a dozen people who found our church through an ad that Bill ran for us on the station. Dozens of other churches can say the same thing, and say more. But who knows the cumulative weight of the fruit born from so many thousands of hours of broadcast? How many Christians have been edified while driving in their cars, listening to Hope FM instead of ESPN radio? The fruit has been enormous.

It all began in Pastor Bill's prayer room. Chuck Smith spoke a word of encouragement that hit Pastor Bill right between the eyes. Years of praying, then years of plodding, have seen the soil bear the fruit. Spiritual gifts operated all along.

Are you open to how the Holy Spirit might use you for His Kingdom? Do you listen carefully to what people in your church say, weighing everything by Scripture, holding fast what is good (1 Thessalonians 5:20-21)? God used the spiritual gifts of one man in Marlton, there with only a few other believers in the 1990s, to get more than 100 kids singing praises to Jesus every day of the school year (you should see the Joyful Noise concerts), and to get 20 or so radio towers blaring praises to His name 24/7. Do you believe that God might be willing to manifest spiritual gifts through you?

Thank you, Pastor Bill, for your encouragement.

Cornerstone Strong—Psalm 95

It's hard to think of a reason to associate salvation with a rock. Rocks are inanimate. They are often in the way. Workers of the field have to clear rocks out of the way in order to bring forth life. Moreover, rocks are sometimes used as instruments of death—the opposite of salvation. Cain was a worker of the field, and it is possible that he picked up a rock and used it to crush the head of Abel. We have already seen that the analogy of crushing with a rock is present in Isaiah 8:14-15 and Luke 20:18, where Christ is the rock that does the crushing. "Rock of salvation" is an odd idea. Yet, it is the crucial object of a prophetic Old Testament song.

Psalm 95 begins with the image of God being a rock that saves. Perhaps there is imagery from the wilderness experience of the Israelites, where God made water come forth from a rock to save the people from death by dehydration (Exodus 17:6). The striking of that rock pictures the death blows delivered to Christ that open a spring of life to us. This image is likely to be the idea of Psalm 95, because the Psalm ends with a warning to the reader not to be like the Israelites who failed to appreciate God's salvation in the wilderness.

Or, instead of looking back to Horeb, perhaps the Psalmist is seeing forward to the Sermon on the Mount (Matthew 7:24-27), where Jesus will compare the building of a life upon His Word to the building of a house on a rock. Flood waters cannot assail it.

Either way, whichever image God meant to evoke by calling Himself "the rock", the image is prophetic of Christ. Moreover, we know that "the rock" certainly connotes strength, and strength not only unassailable but also made available, as the Lord God extends His strong arm to save needy people. Those saved by the Rock are full of praise.

"Oh come, let us sing to the Lord; let us make a joyful noise to the rock of our salvation!" (Psalm 95:1).

Those who have been saved by the Rock become singers. We hear that exhortation repeated in the verse that follows (Psalm 95:2). But the saved don't *just* sing. We must sing *joyfully*. Joyful emotions are commanded more than once in the Psalm (95:1-2). Then, after a reminder of God's greatness and His sovereignty (95:3-5), we are commanded to be *reverent* in our worship (95:6-7). Finally, in verses 8-11, we are warned against irreverence, joylessness, and lack of singing by the example of those who fell in the wilderness.

The charismatic gifts are good and useful, as long as they remain upon the Rock of our salvation. Take them off His Word (Matthew 7:24-27) and they become problematic. But, corresponding to the songs, the joy, and the reverence of Psalm 95, built upon the Rock, the use of the charismatic gifts needs to be doxological, dependent, and delimited.

Doxological

The charismatic gifts have a doxological purpose. That is, they exist to bring glory to the Rock of our salvation. *A doxology* is a hymn, or psalm, or praise to God. We find them sprinkled throughout the Bible, for example in Romans 11:33-36, Jude 24-25, and Revelation 1:5-7. Likewise, Psalm 95, which describes God as the rock of our salvation, is doxological.

Spiritual gifts do not exist to glorify the person through whom they operate. They exist to glorify the name of Jesus. In 1 Corinthians 12:1-3, before really getting into what the gifts are, Paul couches the conversation in a doxological concern. The gifts exist to inspire praise, that people would joyfully and reverently proclaim the truth that "Jesus is Lord" (1 Corinthians 12:3).

As soon as so-called spiritual gifts begin to direct people to delight in the messenger (in his "anointing" or in "what a mighty man of God" he is), the glory is being misdirected. Now, we recognize, people are prone to do that, which is not always the fault of the one with a gift. People did that to Paul and Barnabas (Acts 14:12). But, like the mere servant of Luke 17:10, those in whom spiritual gifts operate need to be very quick to deflect praise. And where titles like "apostle", "great man of God", "God's anointed" (don't touch him!), or "general" are thrown around, there is reason to be concerned that glory is being misdirected and the display of charismaticism is not genuinely from God. Strong gifts are doxological.

Dependent

A second thing we learn, both from Psalm 95 and 1 Corinthians 12-14, is that charismatic gifts are for the edification of the body. They operate dependently within the church, not disconnected from it. That is not to say that gifts cannot operate in privacy. But, even in that unique case of praying in an unknown language when by oneself (1 Corinthians 14:18-19), the priority is for the person to be edified, then to come out from the private place and focus on edifying the body. And what makes one gift more preferable than others is the higher degree to which the preferable gift edifies the church (1 Corinthians 12:31). Love is more excellent than charismatic gifts, carte blanc, because love benefits others, not just oneself.

Notice in Psalm 95 that the invitation for "us" to come is repeated 4 times in the first 2 verses. The body, not just an individual, is beckoned to come. Notice also that we are invited to come sing. The spiritual gifts are especially suited for the gathering of the body in worship. God often raises up great singers to facilitate the singing of the church. And this is a large part of how He builds his church! Most of the churches around the world that we would say are thriving (true and growing) are churches that have joyful singing when they gather, usually led by a singer who has a special gift in that area. Yes, there are talented singers out there on their own. But something special, some spiritual gifts operate, when the church comes together, dependent on each other to help stir up worship. "Oh come!" (Psalm 95) say the gifted ones to the congregation. Strong gifts are dependent.

Delimited

The Bible gets to determine the limits or boundaries of the spiritual gifts. We can't just do extra-biblical stuff simply because we think it helps us accomplish the Great Commission. Anything that the Bible prohibits is obviously out of bounds. For example, when Christians go to the graves of dead Christians and lay down there, hoping to absorb some of that anointing, the practice is out of bounds. Sure, something supernatural happened with the bones of Elisha (2 Kings 13:21), but the many prohibitions against contacting the dead (1 Samuel 28) pushes it out of bounds. Praying in tongues without an interpreter is likewise delimited by the Scripture (1 Corinthians 14:28).

It is not only the explicitly prohibited that we should avoid. Something of the Regulative Principle needs to be observed. Things like slaying in the Spirit, fire tunnels, and various other strange manifestations that never appear in the writings of the apostles need to be avoided, because the Scriptures commend order, decency, and self-control (1 Corinthians 14:26-40).

Psalm 95 is instructive again. "Oh come let us worship and bow down; let us kneel before the Lord, our Maker!" (95:6). Christian worship must be *reverent*. Only reverent worship is worthy to be placed upon the Rock of our salvation. And that delimitation considered, let the overly reserved type of Christian recognize that bowing, kneeling, and even prostrating are prescribed in the Bible! The Greek word for "worship" (proskuneo) more literally means to prostrate oneself. It can be appropriate, if all modesty is protected, to bow, knee and lay oneself out in humility before God. The key is to worship like the worshippers we see in the Bible, while at the same time heeding the delimitations of the Bible.

Application

Just because the Spirit will give spiritual gifts to whomever He pleases (He distributes according to God's will, not ours) doesn't mean we shouldn't eagerly desire and ask for them. God is sovereign over the distribution of gifts (1 Corinthians 12:11), yet we are commanded to "earnestly desire the higher gifts" (1 Corinthians 12:31).

The Christian who is not only careful, but is actually dismissive of the charismatic gifts, will actually be the worse off for it. In all areas of our life, if we ignore portions of Scripture, then we lose out on something. God's secret will is not threatened by this. But His prescribed will included the admonition to "pursue love, and earnestly desire the spiritual gifts, especially that you may prophesy" (1 Corinthians 14:1). We pursue spiritual gifts by asking God for them. I encourage you to do so.

As you do, be sure to remain doxological, dependent, and delimited in your use of spiritual gifts. Do everything to the glory of Jesus Christ (1 Corinthians 10:31), never to attract a following to yourself. Do everything for the edification of the church (1 Corinthians 12:7), never merely to benefit yourself. Do everything within the parameters revealed in Scripture (especially 1 Peter 4, Ephesians 4, Romans 12, and 1 Corinthians 12-14), never simply because it seems to be the emotionally pleasing or pragmatic thing to do.

Give special attention to spiritual gifting when the church gathers. The singing part of the service (Psalm 95) and the preaching part of the service (1 Timothy 4:2) require the operation of spiritual gifts. We need to be growing in these giftings (1 Timothy 4:14-15). Let the worship service be full of singing, full of joy, and completely reverent. Let the use of spiritual gifts be doxological, dependent, and delimited.

Discussion Questions

What do we stand to learn from Pastor Bill's experience in starting Hope FM, developing the Christian School, and building the Church? How were spiritual gifts involved?

What are some of the charismatic errors you have seen? What non-charismatic errors have likewise crept into the church?

How does being more or less filled with the Spirit (Ephesians 4:30, 5:18) affect the degree to which the spiritual gifts operate in our lives? Do you know Christians whom God seems to use in especially strong ways?

How does prayer relate to spiritual gifts? Are there things that Christians do not have because we fail to ask for them? What are some things for which you asked that the Lord finally provided? Is it a threat to God's secret will to ask for things according to His prescribed will?

What does it mean to say that the spiritual gifts must always be used doxologically? Have you seen positive or negative examples?

What does it mean to say that the spiritual gifts must always be used dependently? How could the gift of tongues edify the body even if it is only practiced by individuals in privacy?

What does it mean to say that the spiritual gifts must always be delimited by Scripture?

Are there any teachings in Scripture about the gifts ceasing at any point before the second coming of Christ? Are there any admonitions to exercise spiritual gifts?

5. STRONG LOVE

"Having purified your souls by your obedience to the truth for a sincere brotherly love, love one another earnestly from a pure heart" (1 Peter 1:22)

"you yourselves like living stones are being built up as a spiritual house, to be a holy priesthood, to offer spiritual sacrifices acceptable to God through Jesus Christ. For it stands in Scripture: "Behold, I am laying in Zion a stone, a cornerstone chosen and precious, and whoever believes in him will not be put to shame" (1 Peter 2:5-6)

Boldly Evangelical, thoroughly Biblical, unapologetically Calvinistic, carefully Charismatic churches amount to nothing if they do not have LOVE (1 Corinthians 13:2). Strong love is the last, and maybe the most important, ingredient of what it takes for a church to thrive in a godless culture.

Rubbing elbows with other believers once a week, on Sunday morning, is not enough. To be strong enough to thrive, a church needs to be in fellowship throughout the week. Individual believers are saved by Christ personally, each one relating individually to Him. But in the very moment of personal salvation, the Holy Spirit baptizes the person into the body of Christ (1 Corinthians 12:13). We are inextricably connected with one another.

The Cornerstone theme helps us here. We are living stones (1 Peter 2:5) built on the Cornerstone, Jesus Christ. With Him as our preeminent stone, we are built up to form *one* house. Like stones stacked upon each other, we are intertwined. A disconnected living stone would be oxymoronic, because the whole house lives and functions as one, giving spiritual worship to our Preeminent. Consider three motifs in 1 Peter 2:5. One, Christ upholds the house that stands on Him. Two, Christ is the Great High Priest standing among us—His order of priests. Three, Christ is the Lamb of God standing among us—living sacrifices. These three motifs of 1 Peter 2:5 all reveal that genuine connection with Christ yields close connection with other believers. By becoming one with Him, we become one building, one Priesthood, one sacrificial community.

The early believers had strong love for one another. "And all who believed were together and had all things in common. And they were selling their possessions and belongings and distributing the proceeds to all, as any had need. And day by day, attending the temple together and breaking bread in their homes, they received their food with glad and generous hearts, praising God and having favor with all the people. And the Lord added to their number day by day those who were being saved" (Acts 2:44-47). Far from Communism (a political invention whereby the government intrudes upon private property and takes command over the economy), the community of early believers was built upon self-giving. Believers sold what belonged to *them*, because they generously desired to meet the needs of others.

Notice also the *daily* involvement in the lives of one another. In America's faster-paced economy, in which we all do well to compete, we may not be able to literally see one another every day. But believers should be assembling somewhere every day, whether it is a deacon visiting the elderly, an elder meeting with a few people for an early morning bible study, or any congregant paying a visit to a church member they love (or would like to get to know). It is the daily involvement of believers in the lives of others that mirrors the behavior of the early church.

Fellowship groups (small groups, care groups, or whatever you want to call them) organized by the church are very helpful ways to facilitate interconnectedness. So are men's meetings, women's meetings, or other meetings, even those that might be built around a common interest (sports ministry, book clubs, singing groups, etc.). The Word of God should be given center stage in these organized gatherings of the church. But the more believers spend time together, especially in a fast-paced culture that seeks to tear us apart, the better.

One of the greatest ways for us to spend time together is to serve together. Nothing forges the relationship of a band of brothers quite like going to war together. When we take on a mission project (renovating a building in the inner city to open a church there, mentoring men who are trying to re-enter society after incarceration, mentoring women who are escaping the snares of drug addiction and prostitution, housing the homeless in our church building a few times a year, going to West Virginia to help poor victims of a flood), we give the strong love of Jesus to hurting people. But we also develop deeper love for one another in the church.

Wanting to encourage greater love in the church, I sat down for an interview with Pastor Marty Berglund. In answer to my questions, he provided the following responses, which I edited [with permission] to distill the core idea—the nuggets for us to take away.

Pastor Marty Berglund, Fellowship Alliance Chapel

Jeff: "How important is love to the thriving of a church?"

Marty: "Love is crucial to everything we do. Love is supposed to be at the core of our motivations."

Jeff: "Does growing bigger mean that the church tends to become less loving?"

Marty: "The wonderful thing about getting bigger is that you can help more people with specific problems. I just met with a couple this morning, before coming here, that lost their daughter. Well, we have an amazing grief ministry here that is able to minister specifically in that area. We weren't able to do that until we were 1500 people. Now, we have a pastor, who has experienced grief in his own life, dedicated to helping those who have a child who died, or a spouse, etc. Ministries like this grief ministry or one we have to those with special needs, become more viable as the church grows."

Jeff: "How do you motivate love?"

Marty: "God forgave me in Christ when I didn't deserve it, and I am supposed to love that way. Believers need to be reminded of that. Also, we must teach that being tenderhearted means being able to see things from another's point of view. Getting into fellowship helps us to understand where others are coming from. We begin to have compassion when we understand them. So, getting people involved in close fellowship, especially in groups, is a key."

Jeff: "How do you get rid of malice, gossip, slander, etc., which can stunt the growth of the church?"

Marty: "You have to go meet with [him or her]. You have to get people focused on the Lord, which means getting them focused on the Word. Even when they are criticizing and complaining, ask them what the Lord is doing in the situation. Also, they need to see you—the leader—focused on the Lord."

Jeff: "How do you get a church to be a holy priesthood, offering spiritual sacrifices...ministering?"

Marty: "I believe in the bond of unity. They need to be in a small group. If your personality type is singular-relational or familial-relational, versus multi-relational *[Marty was referencing a certain personality test]*, you may not be ministering to every newcomer that comes into the building, but you can minister in a smaller setting. Some will have the personality to minister to everyone who walks through the door. These may be the evangelists in the church. But everyone can be in a small group and minister there."

Jeff: "How do we spur on love both here and abroad?"

Marty: "Think locally, regionally, and globally, according to Acts 1:8. Then form teams. A good coach brings the best out of you. That's a lot of what love does. That's a lot of what the New Testament "one anothers" are about. Recognize in other believers that the Holy Spirit is in there.

Bring together groups. Take a team approach. Sit down with the team and listen to ideas. Empower others to step out in ministry."

Thank you, Pastor Marty, for your encouraging words.

Cornerstone Strong—1 Peter 2

The three most important Old Testament passages, when it comes to the Cornerstone theme, are Psalm 118:22, Isaiah 28:16, and Isaiah 8:14. Peter quotes all three of them, in rapid-fire succession. Pretty good for an uneducated fisherman (Acts 4:13).

Peter quotes them to develop his theme of shame and rejection. Christ was put to shame in being rejected by Israel. Likewise, we Christians ought to expect to be shamed and rejected as we identify with Christ. But take heart. The various trials last for a little while (1 Peter 1:6) but ultimately result in "praise and glory and honor at the revelation of Jesus Christ" (1:7).

In the Cornerstone analogy, the builders (Israel's leaders) reject Jesus Christ, thinking him unfit to serve as the cornerstone of God's house. But the one rejected by men is "in the sight of God chosen and precious" (2:4). Israel's leaders press forward and build their own edifice, preferring whatever else they choose for their cornerstone. Meanwhile, God builds upon Jesus, and we (His Church) "like living stones are being built up as a spiritual house" (2:5). Anyone who believes that Jesus Christ is, in truth, God's Cornerstone "will not be put to shame" (2:6). "So the honor is for you who believe" (2:7). The temporary shaming and rejection of Christ and His children finds resolution in the ultimate honor that is afforded to Christ, which He, in turn, shares with us.

In Peter's apostolic writing, the Cornerstone analogy points to the final glorification of the very one who suffered shame and rejection. The glory of Christ is displayed in the Church. We ourselves (2:5), built together as one building, standing upon the once-rejected now-exalted stone are a glorious edifice. We are a monument to His greatness. But we don't just stand there. The analogy shifts. Now Peter says that the spiritual house is also "a holy priesthood"— the active agents who serve inside the house. We "offer spiritual sacrifices acceptable to God through Jesus Christ" (2:5). We need to look to the context of 1 Peter to learn what those sacrifices are, what it is that living stones actually do to bring honor to Jesus Christ.

Purified

This Cornerstone pericope (1 Peter 2:4-8) actually begins 7 verses earlier. Peter's train of thought carries him into his discourse on rejection, shame and honor. Peter doesn't just drop the Cornerstone analogy there randomly. Peter had been talking about how the blood of Christ purifies a people and how these people were made "for a sincere brotherly love" (1:22). When Peter brings up the shamed and rejected cornerstone, it is to contrast how Christians ought to treat one another vis a vi how the world treats Christians. The Church needs to love the Church.

Sadly, in our day, it has actually become popular among Christians to dump garbage on the Church. Very often we read church websites that boast about how their new movement has it right. "Traditional churches do X, but we do Y". Fill in the blank with emerging church concepts, missional church concepts, or whatever the newest wave happens to be. They love to trash the Church. They rail against "mega-churches" (as if large numbers necessarily implies superficiality), or "small churches" (as if small numbers necessarily implies inadequacy), and the formality of "religious" churches (as if religion and relationship are necessarily at odds with each other).

The sad part is that Christians are very willing to throw other Christians under the bus. I'm talking about the Stone-Campbell Syndrome (we are the restored church), or what's popular in our day, the cult-like superiority syndrome of ordinary Christians who think it's ok to bash other churches.

Peter will say that there is only one spiritual house. There are many living stones, but there is one house (2:5). Cults aren't a part of it, because they believe in a different Jesus, whereas there is only one "chosen and precious" Cornerstone. But whether a Christian is Baptist, Independent, Sovereign Grace, Calvary Chapel, Christian and Missionary Alliance, or Evangelical Free (all of which are represented in this book), if you are *purified*, you are part of the one body.

For Peter, the issue is whether or not a person has been *purified*. And if so, Peter's exhortation is to "love one another earnestly from a pure heart" (1:22). Being "born again" (1:23) happens when a person repents and believes "the good news that was preached to you" (1:25). Those who have been born again are as different from those who have not as a different house is from the true Temple of the living God. The purified are required to give special honor to the purified. If you belong to the Church, be careful how you conduct yourself in the household of God. Honor one another. Make sure you have strong love for all who have been purified.

Peaceable

In practical terms, having "strong love" means that we are required to be very peaceable. It means that we are to be pleasant to be around, without sharp elbows, without shrill voices. When the congregation gathers to discuss a given topic, the conversation should be so salty (it should taste so good) that if an unbeliever were a fly on the wall, they would have no grounds for disparaging us. Peaceable words that seek to edify the church, not poison darts that seek to kill anyone who stands in the way, ought to be your M.O., "if indeed you have tasted that the Lord is good" (2:3).

"So put away all malice and all deceit and all hypocrisy and envy and all slander" (1 Peter 2:1).

Those 5 things are the poison darts that kill a church. It is natural for a church to thrive when members of it are "like newborn infants" (1 Peter 2:2). As long as they get their milk (2:2), which is the pure teaching of the Word of God, believers will be growing. And as we mature, we reproduce ourselves, in the sense of making new believers by preaching the same good news that was preached to us (1:25). Believers growing up into salvation, and new believers being born as we grow, is the ordinary course of events. But the sad reality is that sometimes things cut in and prevent growth. Like car accidents, diseases, depression, or financial disaster in the world, so also do things cut in on the church and stunt our growth, breaking the ordinary flow of our thriving.

Malice, deceit, hypocrisy, envy, and slander are the opposite of peaceable behavior. These things generally encroach upon the church through a few individuals and a thousand words. The apostle James warns that "the tongue is a small member, yet it boasts of great things" (3:5). He then demonstrates how small things, like a bit in the mouth of a horse, or a ship's rudder, or a small spark of fire, can make a huge impact. A horse can be turned. An entire ship can be turned. Or an entire forest can be turned into ashes by mere words! Thriving churches must guard carefully against malice, deceit, hypocrisy, envy, and slander. One gossipy person can ruin a reputation, and the Church is greatly harmed when that happens. Strong love is peaceable.

Priestly

But strong love is not only about what we don't do. Love is active. Strong love is very active. In Peter's usage of the Cornerstone analogy, the Temple that rises upon Christ is not an empty building. It is an active house of worship. It is a place of "spiritual sacrifice" (2:5). There is a "holy priesthood" at work in the building. And the near context in 1 Peter implies what that work is.

To "love one another earnestly" (1:22) does not mean to sit quietly in a corner contemplating how much affection we have for each other. The Priesthood offering sacrifices in the Temple (2:5) is not a sentimental image. It is, rather, active and involved, even gruesome. The work of the Priest makes his hands dirty.

When members of a church *love one another earnestly*, we get involved in one another's lives. When one of our own is bleeding, we get our hands dirty applying bandages. If some can't work because their body is broken, those who can work need to work a little harder, in order to have a little extra to help our brothers and sisters in need. We make time for a phone call. We make meals for the sick. We make it the very work of our lives to serve our family.

But that service is not only physical, nor even is it especially physical, but rather, it is *spiritual*. God finds our "spiritual sacrifices" acceptable to God through Jesus Christ (2:5). Spiritual sacrifices involve the investment of real and tangible things, like time, talent and treasure, but they are given for spiritual purposes. To devote time, to contribute talent, or to give money to some work of the church that aims to glorify Jesus Christ is to make a "spiritual sacrifice". We learned earlier that the exercise of our spiritual gifts needs to be *doxological*. In the same way, everything we give should ultimately be given for the glory of Jesus Christ. Strong love is priestly.

Application

The most practical way to make a spiritual sacrifice is to go to church and love the people with whom you gather. First of all, do so on the morning of the first day of the week. Gather every Sunday morning, the Lord's Day (kuria hemera), the day that belongs to Him (Revelation 1:10), and encourage every fellow believer with whom you gather. Ask them about themselves. Ask how goes their walk with Christ. Place your hand on their shoulder and pray with them, right there in the hall. You are a Priest, and this is your spiritual sacrifice.

Second, be involved with at least one other gathering of your church throughout the week. Join a care group. By gathering together with a smaller band of brothers and sisters, you will have the time to really get involved in the lives of a few. At times Jesus gathered with thousands. But more often, He had 12 disciples into whom He poured His time and energy. Sometimes He would go even smaller than that, gathering with Peter, James, and John, making spiritual sacrifices of love in their lives.

Finally, love those who are outside the church as well. Scripture commends giving priority (in terms of devoting time, talent and treasure) to those inside the church (Galatians 6:10). But we must not forget "all men" (6:10). For some, it's just easier to *only* take time for our own (Matthew 5:46-47). But the love God has shed abroad in our hearts (Romans 5:5) is big. He can multiply our time to make us available to give love to the world, meeting needs where we can. Love doesn't mean affirming sin (love emptied of truth is not sincere—1 Peter 1:22), but it does mean having compassion for those who are suffering. We can even meet some of their physical needs, always remembering that their greatest need is spiritual. Try to meet that need by offering a spiritual sacrifice. Offer them "the living and abiding word of God" (1 Peter 1:23).

The famous love chapter of the Bible (1 Corinthians 13) places love in a preeminent place, over faith, hope, and the usage of spiritual gifts (1 Co. 12-14). The same goes for this chapter of this book. We saved love for last, not because it is least important, but because it is preeminent. Churches that desire to thrive in this godless culture in which we live must be full of purified people who live peaceably together and "love one another earnestly from a pure heart" (1 Peter 1:22).

Discussion Questions

What do you and your church need to learn from what Pastor Marty had to say?

How do rejection, shame and honor play into Peter's development of the Cornerstone motif?

Have you noticed a trend where Christians are quick to dump garbage on the Church? How can we show honor to other churches who are purified by the blood of Jesus, even if there are minor differences in doctrine or methodology?

Do you think there is a special obligation for Christians to earnestly love those who have been purified?

How important is it for Christians to be peaceable? How dangerous are malice, deceit, hypocrisy, envy, and slander in a church?

What does it mean to be Priestly? What are some examples of "spiritual sacrifices" (1 Peter 2:5) that the "holy Priesthood" (2:5) are to offer?

In what tangible ways does your "sincere brotherly love" (1 Peter 1:22) need to get stronger?

CONCLUSION

I close with the words of the old hymn writer, Samuel J. Stone, interjecting my own words where they fit. This book is merely an echo of what others have said and a reminder of what we need to continue to be in order to thrive in this godless generation.

"The Church's one foundation
is Jesus Christ her Lord;
she is his new creation *(Evangelical)*
by water and the Word. *(Biblical)*
From heaven he came and sought her
to be his holy bride
with his own blood he bought her,
and for her life he died. *(Calvinistic)*
Elect from every nation,
yet one o'er all the earth;
her charter of salvation,

one Lord, one faith, one birth;
one holy name she blesses,
partakes one holy food,
and to one hope she presses,
with every grace endued. *(Charismatic)*
Though with a scornful wonder *(Loving)*
we see her sore oppressed,
by schisms rent asunder,
by heresies distressed,
yet saints their watch are keeping;
their cry goes up, "How long?"
and soon the night of weeping
shall be the morn of song.
Mid trial and tribulation,
and tumult of her war,
she waits the consummation
of peace forevermore;
till, with the vision glorious,
her longing eyes are blest,
and the great church victorious
shall be the church at rest.

ABOUT THE AUTHOR

Jeff Kliewer is the Pastor of Cornerstone Church—
an Evangelical Free church in Mt. Laurel, New Jersey.
He is a Dallas Theological Seminary graduate. He is
married, with two children. From 2004 to 2016, he
and his family served as missionaries to inner-city
Philadelphia. His ambition is to know Christ and
labor for a lifetime to see Christ's Church rise upon
Him—our great Cornerstone.

Made in the USA
Middletown, DE
21 November 2017